Elizabeth R. Skoglund

More Precious Than a Sparrow

More Precious Than a Sparrow
© 2013 by Elizabeth R. Skoglund.
Published by Netmenders.
All rights reserved.

Cover design by John Whorrall Jr.

ISBN: 978-0-615-92458-8

Library of Congress Control Number: 2013921561

No part of this publication may be reproduced, stored in a retrieval system, or transmitted in any form or by any means – electronic, mechanical, photocopy, recording, or any other except for brief quotations in printed reviews – without the prior permission of the publisher.

Printed in the United States of America.

TABLE OF CONTENTS

1. More Precious Than a Sparrow......................13
2. Free Coffee..17
3. Twenty-four Hours 21
4. Hot Coffee and Cold Lemonade 24
5. The Transition 28
6. Normal Day...31
7. A Miracle 34
8. One Small Candle....................................37
9. The Star 40
10. Remembering...45
11. Unconditional Love..................................48
12. Half a Pie..52
13. Foxhole in the Mind 55
14. In His Time 60
15. A Declaration of Meaning...........................64
16. Wonder Years 69
17. No Throwaway Years................................73
18. Starting at the End 78
19. The Rescue..81

20.	Most Precious Possession	84
21.	Small Things	88
22.	The Red Geranium	92
23.	Just to Be	96
24.	Positive Rage	99
25.	Small Occasions of Relief	103
26.	Gingerbread Boys	107
27.	Love Letters	110
28.	Freedom	115
29.	An Orange, a Photo, an Email	118
30.	The Price Tag of One Life	122
31.	The Good Report	127
32.	Early Arrival	129
33.	I'll Never Again Be Anyone's Child	132
34.	Angels Unaware	137
35.	Only Eighteen Hours	141
36.	Images on Easter, 1999	144
37.	Pink Clouds	147
38.	A Different Clientele	152
39.	The Martyr	156
40.	The Safety Zone of Christmas	159
41.	The Stranger	163
42.	Reaching Earth	166

TABLE OF CONTENTS

43. Untrod Territory 170
44. The Lesson of the Tide 175
45. Messiah 179

For Elizabeth Hannah, with love.

Do not two sparrows sell for a halfpenny? Yet not one of them will fall to the ground without your Father's leave. But as for you, the very hairs on your heads are all numbered. Away then with fear; you are more precious than a multitude of sparrows.

— Matthew 10: 29-31 (*Weymouth*)

Acknowledgements

Few if any books are produced in solitude. The material for *More Precious Than a Sparrow* came over the years, filtered by time but also influenced, both in interpretation and choice, by people like Viktor Frankl, Pamela Reeve, G. L. Harrington, C. S. Lewis, Ruth Bell Graham and Amy Carmichael, just to cite a few. Much gratitude is extended to Lance Wilcox for his handling of the technological aspects of publishing this book and for his editorial and proofreading skills, which enhanced the book incredibly, and to John Whorrall Jr. for creating a cover which with one image captures the essence of the entire book. My thanks to Rayne and Elizabeth Wilcox for their practical help and encouragement and to Elizabeth for writing the back copy. Much appreciation goes to those who prayed, especially Rayne Wilcox and the ladies in Netmenders.

- 1 -

More Precious Than a Sparrow

I once met a remarkable fish! At first glance he was just an ordinary goldfish, swimming around in his bowl full of seaweed and other goldfish accoutrements. As he flipped his fins and turned around at the edge of the bowl, he looked healthy and beautiful. Then someone pushed a button, and the goldfish blew a kiss. I discovered that the seaweed and thermometer had appeared in the "tank" as rewards for taking good care of the fish. The owner had simply gone to bed and found each of them there the next morning, to her surprise automatically produced by the computer. The goldfish wasn't a goldfish at all. He was part of a computer app, a sort of virtual reality fish. He dies and actually floats to the top like any other goldfish if he is not properly taken care of. You feed him, and if you go away for a week and leave him unattended he will die. Yet he was never alive, for he is not a real goldfish.

As I looked at him gracefully swimming around I wondered how a child would view him. Would it make some children confused about the very definition of life? Would some begin to feel that nothing is real and so no life is really all that precious? At worst will the whole concept of virtual reality degrade the concept of the preciousness of life? After all, video games which involve using human beings for target practice look every bit as real as the goldfish and do an excellent job of making people desensitized to killing. To explain further the effect of virtual reality on children, I asked one young computer expert what he thought about my "virtual" goldfish? "He's as real as any other goldfish," he responded. "I don't see much difference." I found out that a number of young people who are deep into cyberspace and the like see only shadowy differences between reality and non-reality.

Yet the other side of virtual reality is that it is in truth NOT reality. It only looks real. The goldfish functions as a robot, by the click of a button, not because it is an intelligent being. Yet that form of robotic being is exactly what God could have made when He decided to create mankind. In contrast, REAL beings are made in the image of God, each with a free will. Even the created animal world moves about as it wishes. That is the miracle of creation.

In the world of virtual reality there is no pain, no joy, no Heaven, no Hell – no real existence, nothing to lose or gain. In the very real world of my counseling office a little girl reminded me of how terrible that unreal world would be. She was only six, but already she had the experience of a lifetime. Abandonment, drugs, beatings: these had replaced hot chocolate and bedtime stories in her childhood thus far.

One day when she walked into my counseling office crying with uncontrollable sobs I was ready for the worst.

"He died," she choked out. "He died!"

Completely bewildered, I gently asked her who had died. It turned out that a small bird had fallen out of its nest, and she had found it on the way home from school. The little creature was way too young to survive such a fall, and even to live on its own. And so he had died quietly in the child's cupped hands. Unlike our fish, good care didn't guarantee success.

"I'm never going to love again!" the child sobbed. Her words reflected her background of pain as much as her grief over the death of the little bird. In this small incident the proverbial straw had broken. We talked about risk and how taking risks always involves the chance that you will be hurt. But without risk you also lose the chance for closeness and love. This is the reality of the real world.

Quietly the child reflected on these thoughts. Then, brushing away her tears she concluded: "I guess it's best to love even if it can hurt. I promise I'll try."

At present we see indistinctly, as in a mirror, but then face to face. At present I know partially; then I shall know fully, as I am fully known.
— 1 Corinthians 13:12 (*New American Bible*)

- 2 -

Free Coffee

It doesn't seem to be that many years ago when I was in my mid thirties and a waitress asked to see my ID before she would serve me wine. At first I thought she was just joking. But when I joked back she didn't look happy. So I jovially handed her my driver's license, validating that I was indeed of age.

Some 30 years later, I stopped at a coffee shop on the way home from having my hair done. I was recovering from a back injury and it was the first time I had been able to go anywhere in quite a few weeks. As I slowly sipped the hot coffee and savored its unusually bracing aroma I felt alive again. Even the warmth of the cup as I wrapped my fingers around it felt comforting and secure.

One cup was not enough, but when I requested a refill the young waitress asked the fateful question: "Are you over 59?" In response to my affirmative answer she informed me: "Then your coffee is free." It seemed like a gesture of dubious value. For the simple price of a cup of coffee I had abandoned youth and become a senior citizen.

Even though an invitation at age 50 to join the AARP

is, for most people, the first distant reminder that age is approaching, I had always considered 65 as the real start of senior citizenship. And in recent years, with increased life expectancy in general, in my mind that number had been increased to 70 or 75.

A few weeks after my coffee incident I picked up a copy of former President Jimmy Carter's book *The Virtues of Aging*. I was delighted to hear that he had experienced a similar betrayal of age through free coffee. He too had turned down an early offer of membership in the AARP because, as he put it, "…we considered ourselves too young to face the stigma of senior citizenship."

Then, however, after leaving the White House the reality of aging caught up with him and was made abruptly clear over a cup of coffee. After stopping for breakfast on a drive midway to Atlanta, Carter noticed that his bill was less than those who accompanied him. When he questioned the amount, thinking a mistake had been made, an older farmer sitting at a nearby table called out in a booming voice: "Your bill ain't no mistake, Mr. President. Before eight o'clock they give free coffee to senior citizens."

So many great truths in life are learned in events of a few seconds duration. A near miss on the highway makes us realize the fragility of life. The little childish voice on the other end of the phone saying "I love you" creates a sense of the brevity and preciousness of those childhood years.

Before that day in the coffee shop I had always been goal oriented. But still life seemed to be a long time, with plenty of time left. Then in less than a minute, for the price of a cup of coffee, I faced aging and the prospect of limited time. Now each day seemed important and life took on a new sense of value because of its uncertainty. Maybe both Jimmy Carter and myself and all the millions of growing-older people who are given free cups of coffee are given more than just coffee. We are given a second chance to value each day, each hour, each minute.

※

Lost, yesterday, somewhere between sunrise and sunset, two golden hours, each set with sixty diamond minutes. No reward is offered for they are gone forever.

— Horace Mann

- 3 -

Twenty-four Hours

A young man had been ill for a long time. Because of his health he had lost his job as well as his money. Since no physician had been able to figure out what was wrong with him, Rob saw little hope for his future. In a last attempt to find a cure, he went to a new specialist who performed additional laboratory tests.

"Just one more useless opinion," Rob muttered under his breath to a friend. "You know he's not going to come up with anything new!"

That night Rob gave up. He killed himself. Twelve hours later the physician called with the test results. Rob had a disease which *untreated* would leave him incapacitated. *Treated* – he could live a normal life.

"May I talk to Rob," the physician asked. "I have great news for him."

There was a long silence. A choked-up voice on the other end of the phone said: "Rob died last night. He killed himself."

Less than twenty-four hours would have made the difference.

The late Catherine Marshall, wife of Senate Chaplain

Peter Marshall, once said that she believed that most people who commit suicide would not do so if they just waited for twenty-four hours. Time heals. Time gives us a chance to put things into perspective. Time gives us opportunity to reach out for help. Time gives us a chance to value what we are about to give up.

⚜ ⚜

There is a time, we know not when,
A point we know not where,
That marks the destiny of men,
For glory or despair.

— Joseph Addison

- 4 -

Hot Coffee and Cold Lemonade

Shortly after our family first moved to California from Chicago, we began attending a large church in downtown Los Angeles. After church we sometimes walked several blocks through the downtown area to a cafeteria that had flowing fountains throughout the building and seemingly endless choices of foods. On our way we almost always encountered a "street beggar." Beggars weren't called "the homeless" in those days, but they were the same as today: displaced, hungry, needy.

Indelibly etched upon my memory is the image of my father sharing what he had with anyone who asked him for help. Sometimes he gave money; sometimes he bought someone a hot cup of coffee. It was never much. We didn't have much. But my father never turned anyone away. He never treated another human being as though they were not worth noticing. And he never handed anyone religious literature instead of food when they were hungry.

Once I heard someone criticize my father when they saw him give money. "How do you know that man won't buy liquor with the money?" the friend concluded. "It's not enough money for liquor," my father replied. "Besides, what he does with the money is up to him. My duty is to try to help." The dignity of that homeless man counted a great deal to my father.

My mother and father were both very generous people who cared about others. When a neighbor was ill, my mother would bring them meals. My mother in particular had a real love for the elderly. Some of my earliest recollections are of being with my parents when they brought flowers and food to some lonely widow.

From World War II I have vague memories of food rationing shared with an immigrant who stayed with us for a brief time. And I remember visiting some Japanese friends in an internment camp and playing with the children there while my parents helped their parents store some of their belongings.

After my mother's death a neighbor told me about a time when she was temporarily bedridden after a serious car accident. It was a hot summer day without air conditioning when my mother arrived with a pitcher full of ice cold lemonade. The neighbor told me how characteristic that had been of my mother and how nothing in her own experience had ever tasted quite as good as that cold lemonade.

I grew up seeing Scripture shaped into shoe leather. My parents put into action principles which guide Christians in doing good. As a result, the words of Jesus to his disciples hold special meaning for me: "For I was hungry and you gave me food, I was thirsty and you gave me drink...ill and you cared for me, in prison and you visited me...whatever you did for one of these least brothers of mine, you did for me." (Matthew 25:35-36, 40, *New American Bible*)

To help those who needed assistance became an automatic way of looking at life. That another person's need brought to my door becomes my obligation was a lesson I learned early, just by watching my parents.

※

Religion that is pure and undefiled before God and the Father is this: to care for orphans and widows in their affliction and to keep oneself unstained by the world.

— James 1:27 (*New American Bible*)

- 5 -

The Transition

A man of eighty sat in my office telling me of his wife to whom he had been married some fifty years. She had developed Alzheimer's and required total care, which this man was trying to give her at home. Taking care of her was not an easy task. She barely recognized him and was often difficult to handle. He was elderly, and the dark circles around his eyes, the drawn look on his face were evidence of the toll his task was taking on him. When I asked him why he didn't put her in a convalescent home, a gentle look came over his face.

"Sometimes I don't know why," he started to explain, "but at night when she's asleep lying in bed next to me, she's herself again. I hold her, and look at her; and I have my wife again for just a little while."

A short time later the woman died suddenly of a heart attack. But by the time she died, her husband had become gradually accustomed to doing without her. During that long transition between earth and Heaven, unknown to her until eternity, she had been a comfort to her grieving husband. She had helped him get used to her dying. When she was asleep she had reminded him of what used to be, and then toward the end she had gradually withdrawn from him during those difficult waking hours when she didn't even recognize him. Even with the worst symptoms of her disease, her life had been meaningful.

※

My times are in thy hand...

— Psalm 31:15 (*King James Version*)

- 6 -

Normal Day

It was a bright, brisk autumn day when I, an eight-year-old child, stood at the end of the Malibu pier with my father and cut up my own bait for fishing. My sister was fifteen, bored with the scene, and away for the day. But for my father and me the sea, the salt breeze blowing on our faces, the smell of fish and the adventure of fishing were all our thing together. And now, as an adult, I still seek out the sea for comfort and strength. However, now it is my thing alone or with a friend because my father is not here.

As a little girl it was a time of one-to-one aloneness with my father. I learned that he and his father built a boat in Chicago and used it on Lake Michigan and that my father was actually born on a ship in the Stockholm harbor. He learned that I could put bait on a hook and really catch a fish, even though I was a girl. We became close in our sharing.

When I was a teenager, I had a remarkable English teacher who possessed a unique appreciation of life. Her name is written in gold letters in my memory: Esther Mildred Weinstock. She used to write quotations on the blackboard, and often I copied them into a notepad that I still have. One such quotation expresses the simple joy of ordinary human life, the kind of time I spent with my father on the pier, and it challenges us to grasp that ordinariness while it still exists:

> Normal day, let me be aware of the treasure you are. Let me learn from you, savor you, bless you before you depart. Let me not pass you by in quest of some rare and perfect tomorrow. Let me hold you while I may, for it will not always be so. One day I shall dig my nails into the earth, or bury my face in the pillow, or stretch myself taut, or raise my hands to the sky, and want more than all the world your return.
>
> — Mary Jane Irion

This is the day the Lord has made; let us be glad and rejoice in it.

— Psalm 118:24 (*New American Bible*)

A MIRACLE

For months the young woman had been undergoing medical tests and then treatment with various medications. As time went on her health began to improve. She felt better. Then with the results of one blood test her world fell apart: she was pregnant and because of all the tests and treatment she had received, the prognosis for the baby was multiple defects and possible early death. The medical recommendation? Abortion.

Viewing a film showing some early ultrasound pictures of a first trimester infant moving to avoid the needle used in an abortion, the pregnant woman decided affirmatively against abortion. She would ask God for a miracle, but she was not naive. She knew that God sometimes says "No." But she also had seen something of the preciousness of human life as she watched the twelve-week-old "fetus" struggle to survive. Her own baby was fifteen weeks old at the time. She could not assault him in that way.

"I can't believe that you are considering having this child just because you believe in some idiot God," an exasperated but highly trained medical specialist said to the mother.

"You're not going to get some miracle," she concluded.

The next months were rough: nightmares of a monster child; wakefulness and cold sweats in the middle of the night; health problems which had improved but still complicated the pregnancy.

Then nine months after the nightmare began, a beautiful and perfectly normal baby boy was born. The miracle had happened. God had said "yes."

Eighteen months later the mother and her toddler stood unannounced in the waiting room of the specialist who had told her not to expect a miracle from her "idiot God."

"May we see Dr. —," the mother asked the receptionist. "It will only take a few minutes. Just tell her I want to show her a miracle."

The doctor appeared in the doorway. "What a wonderful little boy!" she exclaimed as she bent down and saw the chubby little boy standing there. Then she looked up and her eyes focused on the mother. After a short gasp of recognition she asked, "Is this the child?" "Yes," said the mother softly.

Silently, tears came down the cheeks of this usually composed professional. Then quietly she said: "Your God truly is a God of Miracles."

> You were there while I was being formed in utter seclusion! You saw me before I was born and scheduled each day of my life before I began to breathe...
>
> — Psalm 139:15-16 (*The Living Bible*)

– 8 –

ONE SMALL CANDLE

On an afternoon drive a number of years ago, a friend of mine saw two nine-year-old boys fighting. One grabbed a large tree branch and began hitting the other over the head. Fearing for the victim's life, my friend stopped her car and ran to break up the fight – just as the police arrived.

My friend was stunned by the cold, smug look on the aggressor's face. It was apparent he had relished beating the other boy, and wasn't at all afraid of the police.

Did she do right in stopping to help? Had the police not arrived, she might have been the second victim. But she did what had to be done.

We should think twice when we're tempted to say, "It's none of my business" or "What I do won't matter anyway." The only valid, biblical reason for not getting involved is that God is directing us to stay clear.

Former Supreme Court Justice David Souter, in his confirmation hearings, was asked about his volunteer service on a hospital board. His reply was striking: "You do it because you're paying your dues. You're in the group that's lucky. And the people in the group that are lucky have an obligation to pay it back."

Most of us are also "lucky," so to speak, blessed just to be living in this country. Most of all, as Christians who know Jesus as Saviour, we owe a debt of gratitude we can never repay.

As we have moved into the next millennium, we can see the effects of darkness all around us. We can curse that darkness and passively wait for Christ's return. Or, since we belong to the Light of the world, we can light one small candle. The choice is ours.

You are the light of the world; a town cannot be hid if built on a hill-top. Nor is a lamp lighted to be put under a bushel, but on the lampstand; and then it gives light to all in the house. Just so let your light shine before all men, in order that they may see your holy lives and may give glory to your Father who is in Heaven.

— Matthew 5:14-16 (*Weymouth*)

- 9 -

The Star

Toward the end of World War II in Budapest, Hungary, a child and her family lived with many others in a Swedish safe house. Anna wasn't Swedish at all. She was Jewish. But since, at the end of the war, the largest intact group of Jews were in Hungary, in his attempt to kill all Jews Hitler focused on Hungary. That made Anna a person at risk. Therefore, her family had moved to this protective house where they were safe. Sometimes Anna wondered how safe they really were. She could still hear bombs falling in the distance and gunfire closer by. And she could never understand why she was forbidden to look out the windows. Sometimes Anna peeked out the window anyway; for she was only seven and she was often curious and always very bored.

In Hungary, by the summer of 1944 the Nazi purge of the Jews was accelerated by the arrival of Adolph Eichmann, Hitler's henchman who was out to make the elimination of the Jews more speedy and more complete. The danger to Anna and her family had increased.

Eichmann's archenemy was a young Swede, Raoul Wallenberg, who was a part of the famous banking family in Sweden but who had already learned that saying "No" to people in a bank was not to be his future calling. A graduate of a college in the United States, he had studied architecture; and as a young man he had traveled between Sweden and Hungary encouraging trade between the two countries. Then the war, as its presence was heightened in Budapest, had changed all that; and Raoul Wallenberg had volunteered to take on diplomatic status in order to save as many Jews as possible. The request for this help came from President Roosevelt to the King of Sweden, since Sweden was a neutral country and as such could still function in Hungary.

In addition to issuing passes which guaranteed protection to those who owned them, the Swedes set up safe houses where protected Jews could live. These were often apartment houses along the Danube. Many families lived together in these houses. The Swedish Legation brought them food and other essentials on a regular basis. Anna heard of names like Raoul Wallenberg and Per Anger, and these people whom she had never met became her heroes.

In the safe house where she lived Anna looked forward to the kind people who came and dropped off food. But they couldn't stay and so the days dragged on. She talked to her doll and to a friendly mouse whom she named Thomas. But Thomas always ran back to his hole.

Anna's mother did a lot of needlework and her father

talked with the other men. They talked long into the night while Anna tried to stay awake and listen. But Anna always fell asleep too soon to learn much about what was happening. Also, Anna was old enough to understand that they were in danger but not old enough to understand the full implication of that danger.

Summer went into fall and fall into winter. The Nazis kept moving Jews out of Budapest to a camp named Auschwitz where they were systematically killed. But Anna and her family stayed in the safe house. Anna dreamed about going to school and living in her own house again. But Mama told her she should be grateful just to be alive and safe.

One day Anna heard the older people talking about the war ending soon. Later that same afternoon Anna heard a noise from outside her upstairs window. Trembling, she peeked out of one side of the window and saw a sight which remained with her for life. Several Nazi soldiers were forcing people to lie down in the snow in the formation of the Jewish Star of David. They were ordered to lie still with their faces down in the snow. Then Anna watched in horror as the soldiers shot each person until all that remained were dead bodies, still forming a star but a star which by this time slowly added a red color to the white snow around it.

Anna sat back down and shook. She couldn't even move for a while. Outside the soldiers left and the sky slowly darkened overhead. One more time Anna looked out the window, down at the blood stained snow beneath. Then she gave a faint gasp as she saw one tiny corner of the star move. Someone was still alive. Anna ran downstairs to her father, who had been a well-respected physician before the Nazis came.

"Papa, Papa," she called quietly: "Come quickly!"

Within minutes three men had slipped out the back door and carried a badly wounded young woman back into the safe house. At great risk to all of their lives, a runner was sent to get some added medical supplies. And in the end the woman survived.

Years after the war Anna, now a wife and mother, reflected back. During those days of hiding, it was against the law to look out the window. It was dangerous to leave a safe house for any reason. But on that night in the winter of 1944 nothing seemed more important than the saving of one life. In some strange way saving that one life had been worth risking the lives of many. So much for the current viewpoint of rationing according to age or so-called worth to the state. So much for "life unworthy of life." History has shown us where that goes.

This is my commandment: love one another as I love you. No one has greater love than this, to lay down one's life for one's friends.

— John 15:12-13 (*New American Bible*)

- 10 -

Remembering

I never met Sister Agnes. I don't remember a first correspondence, except that every now and then when I would publish a new book a letter would come telling me how she used the book to help someone or to teach a class for young mothers.

Then the car accident happened and I lost my mother as a result. "She was old and lived a good life" conventional wisdom dictated. "One just goes on" was a view even I adhered to. But for me the void was there from the absence of that one life. I would pick up the phone to share a thought and then hang up with the fresh realization that she wasn't there. For me the loss was infinite. I would heal but there would always be a scar.

It was then that the letters from Sister Agnes began to stand out. For years – long after I had adjusted to my mother's death – the letters came, always like clockwork on the day of my mother's death. They provided a marker, a signpost that said, "I remember, I care, and you do not need to feel guilty about remembering so long after the event."

Then one year the letters stopped. August 13 came and went. In all of her vitality Sister Agnes was older than she had seemed in her letters. And so now there was a new void on earth, and Heaven was a little richer still. Someone said she was now walking with God. But another said, with equal correctness, that she had always walked with God.

I never met Sister Agnes. I will have to wait until I get to Heaven for that. Until then I will not forget the impact of her life on mine: the preciousness of human life and the comfort of remembering.

⚜

And thou shalt remember all the way which the Lord thy God led thee...

— Deuteronomy 8:2 (*King James Version*)

- 11 -

Unconditional Love

A young couple who had applied to the Department of Adoptions had specified their willingness to adopt an older, even "special needs," child. "Special needs" meant that the child would have problems. In their minds they imagined things like diabetes, or hyperactivity, or the need for eye surgery. They were somewhat unprepared for what they were to hear.

"The good news is we have an eight-year-old child for you. She's bright. She looks a little like both of you, with her hazel eyes and long, silky brown hair. The bad news is that she's so damaged that she is in need of immediate psychiatric hospitalization. I would advise you to wait for someone else," the social worker concluded.

Steve and Julie Johnson met Suzanne that afternoon in the home where she had been temporarily placed. She was beautiful, but she was also disturbed. The prognosis for the future was a lot of professional help. For a time, at least, the ideal happy family would not exist. There would be a lot of hard work with little short-term results. Even long term, there were no guarantees. She might spend her life in a mental hospital.

As the couple drew closer to Suzanne, Julie reached out a hand and said, "Hello." No response. It was then that they noticed the distant look in her eyes. She didn't really see them – or hear them. She was basically out of reality.

"She doesn't know you're here," said the social worker. "When she came to us she had been beaten a lot and left in a dark room. She learned to escape by leaving reality and that escape doesn't seem as temporary as we had first hoped. That's why she needs more treatment than we can give her as an outpatient."

A look of understanding passed between the Johnsons. Then Steve said: "We've talked this over. If she's going into a mental hospital, at least she can go with our name. For better or worse we want to adopt her. Everyone should belong. Everyone should have someone who loves them, no matter what." Then turning to the child he said: "We want to be your Mommy and Daddy." The child didn't respond, but they hoped she understood.

It was some months later on a Saturday afternoon when Steve and Suzanne walked hand in hand across the rolling green lawn of the hospital where Suzanne was being treated. Then almost spontaneously the two dropped down on the lawn under a big shady tree. It was summer and a soft warm breeze passed through the leaves of the tree. Suzanne still hadn't talked or even appeared to recognize anyone. Yet she seemed to enjoy them when either of the Johnsons visited.

Turning to Suzanne, Steve picked up a leaf and said, "It's pretty, isn't it?" No response. But then Suzanne did something she had not done before. She turned and looked straight at Steve. For the first time her face registered expression. Then slowly, looking into his eyes, she said: "I see you in my eyes, Daddy."

"Welcome home," said Steve softly, as he gently gave her a hug.

⇥ ⇤

You didn't seem to do a thing but be there. And yet a harbor doesn't do anything either, except to stand there with arms always outstretched, waiting for the traveler to come home.

— Virginia Axline

- 12 -

HALF A PIE

It was a cold Midwestern morning when George faced his first day as a history professor at a local college. Far away in the sunny West his family prepared to wait until Spring before they pulled up their roots and joined him. Right now as George gulped down a cup of quickly cooling coffee and listened to the silence around him, he wondered if he should have taken his family with him right away.

Once at work he cheered up. At least there were people, friendly people, around him. Later in the day, as he left the building to go home, an older faculty member approached him. "Do you like homemade pie?" she asked a little abruptly. Taken by surprise, George answered, "Why yes, I do." Pleased, she handed him a pie tin with half a pie in it. Then she hurried away.

That night as George finished off the last crumb of pie with, this time, a cup of steaming hot coffee, he thought about the older lady and what he had learned about her from a friend. Her husband had died a year before, and so she had lost the one person for whom she had baked for 30 years. But instead of withdrawing into self pity, she now baked for all kinds of lonely people who not only enjoyed the results of her culinary skills but were cheered up by her kindness as well.

"You go to a strange little town and find there are people with hearts of gold everywhere," George said to himself as he picked up his plate and fork and brought them into the kitchen. Spring didn't seem so far away anymore.

※

Do not keep the alabaster boxes of your love and tenderness sealed up until your friends are dead. Fill their lives with sweetness. Speak approving, cheering words while their ears can hear them and while their hearts can be thrilled by them.

— Henry Ward Beecher

- 13 -

FOXHOLE IN THE MIND

This weekend our family took a vacation. We never left home, but then again we did. It was Memorial Day weekend with the usual traffic and overcrowded hotels and amusements spots. "What would we like to do most?" we asked ourselves. "Scrapbooking!" was the spontaneous answer. And so, scrapbook we did.

Genealogical searches through the Internet, stamping, journaling, cropping pictures: all these were the tools of our trade. Reminiscing about what we've done and where we've been also contributed to the event. With new colored pencils, stamps, and ink pads we produced many scrapbook pages, each filled with photos, written comments and memories. At the end we wondered at how many pages we had finished and how many good times we had remembered.

Amazingly, at the end of two and a half days of turned off phones and ignored mail we had truly been on our own journey into the past. Armed with decent food along with special treats of Rice Krispy squares and coffee coolers, we had been in another world of remembering and recording. At the end we had been away, and to go to work the next day seemed as difficult to adjust to as any other time when we've physically gone away and come back home to once again face the responsibilities of life.

Life is too precious not to refuel in order to go on. Yet sometimes one simply cannot physically leave and go away. But by turning off the sound of the phone and by leaving the mail in the mailbox, anyone can get a short reprieve. A friend of mine once confessed that when he's really feeling world weary, he lets his mail stack up on his desk for a couple of days and ignores the world while he refurbishes. Personally, once I see the mail I have to look at it. So I need to leave it in the mailbox.

There are also short, daily ways to refurbish. For me, reading a mystery book at night after everyone's gone home or to bed can cut the tape of the day. For others, a historical novel or any number of different books accomplish the same thing. "How can I pay my bills?" or "What if I don't meet my deadline?" or "What if my child gets a bad report card?" are all common negative tapes that can dissolve in the quietness and diversion that accompany a good read. For some, needle work, a video or a conversation with a good friend can have a similar effect. Each of these is a mini vacation without leaving home. Each refurbishes and enables one to do one's task just that much more efficiently.

As Christians we have an added option of mini

refurbishment – time alone with God, for God's presence goes with us wherever we go. From the depths of the Nazi concentration camp Corrie Ten Boom could declare that no pit is so deep that He is not deeper still. But God is with us in ordinary life too. In his last legacy to the world before he died, Cardinal Bernardin wrote: "…I promised God and myself that I would give the first hour of each day to prayer…" Then, again, "…early on, I made another decision. I said, 'God, I know that I spend a certain amount of that morning hour of prayer daydreaming, problem-solving, and I'm not sure that I can cut that out. I'll try, but the important thing is, I'm not going to give that time to anyone else.'" That last line has revolutionized my own time with God to the point where I can look forward to my talks with God before the day starts. That is when I once again separate away from the pressures of life, and sort things out with God in a way which brings peace and an ability to go on with a sense of perspective and enablement.

During World War II President Harry Truman was asked how he handled the stress of leadership at that time. His rather unique reply was that he had a foxhole in his mind, a memory of a quiet scene which transported him away from the stress to an inner place of tranquility whenever he needed it. For me, that place is the sea, a specific place where the tide comes in and out and the waves crash against the rocks. The scene reminds me of God's steadfastness and permanence. The ability to have a foxhole in your mind is the ultimate instant vacation, available wherever we find ourselves. That ability is a sort of portable getaway which we all carry around with us.

※

But though my wing is closely bound,
My heart's at Liberty;
My prison walls cannot control
The flight, the freedom of the soul.

— Jeanne Guyon

- 14 -

In His Time

My Aunt Lydia was the last of my close family members to die, and so she was precious to me in a very special way. She had almost died in the car accident that took my mother's life. She had endured the pain of three hip fractures. Her osteoporosis was so bad that her x-rayed bones looked like transparent tissue paper. Yet at the age of eighty-nine she still walked.

On the evening of her death, she was not like she had been all those other times when she had come so close to death. Each time before when she would say, "I think I'm going home to be with the Lord," it seemed right to disagree with her and encourage her to try to live. On this evening, however, as I approached her bed she opened her eyes and said decisively, "I'm dying."

Just that. And I knew she was right.

Yet a few minutes later, when a nurse came in and asked if I wanted a "no code" put on her chart, I panicked. I didn't want to stop fighting for her to live, and I fervently wished for the old days when people just died because there was nothing else medical science could do for them.

My immediate reaction was anger that I was the only one left to decide this. I longed for my family. Perhaps I could simply decide not to decide. But I knew that not to decide was in reality to decide that Aunt Lydia might be kept alive artificially long after her time had come.

But then wasn't that what medicine was supposed to do – keep people alive for as long as possible?

In my confusion, I went to a little coffee shop that had been a retreat for my friends and me as teenagers. In my booth, a small island in the middle of screaming children and rushing adults, I thought and I prayed. I knew I didn't have much time. She would soon stop breathing, and my decision would be made for me. Without the "no code" they would pound and break those brittle bones with CPR. Perhaps they would put her on a respirator to breathe for her – a machine which at that time could not be turned off without a court order.

I find that often when I need God's guidance in the most complicated issues, I get the simplest answers. With a deep sense of calm, I suddenly realized that the decision was not whether or not my aunt should live – it was whether or not to prolong her dying. She was dying. All medical science could do was to painfully prolong that process. And so I decided not to intrude into God's timing for her death.

Within seconds of my conveying to the doctor my decision

not to interfere, Aunt Lydia stopped breathing and was with her Lord. It was *His* time.

You saw me before I was born and scheduled each day of my life before I began to breathe. Every day was recorded in your Book!

— Psalm 139:16 (*The Living Bible*)

- 15 -

A Declaration of Meaning

The place was Berkeley, California, a university town often thought of as liberal and vocal in its views. The time was a weekend in the early seventies. The event was the presentation of a play written by the now late psychiatrist Dr. Viktor Frankl within three years of Frankl's release from the Nazi concentration camps. For me it was one of the most memorable weekends of my life.

Two friends and I flew up to Berkeley for the weekend, which included not only attending the play but meeting people like Dr. Frankl and spending some time with friends.

Viktor Frankl was the feature of the weekend, however. A survivor of Hitler's concentration camps, Buchenwald, Dachau, and Auschwitz, Dr. Frankl, a psychiatrist from Vienna, had devoted his life to the promotion of his psychological message of Logotherapy, a therapy of meaning. For he had discovered in the concentration camps that you can endure any *how* if you know the *why* of your existence. Suffering cannot be eradicated from this earth, but meaning can make suffering endurable.

Prior to this weekend, I had read most of what Frankl had

written, and he had influenced me profoundly as a young psychotherapist. His message of meaning fit right into my own commitment to Christ as my meaning and focus in life. Therefore, just meeting him was a pleasure, and when he took time to ask about my own books and borrowed them for an evening, I was thrilled, particularly when his response to them was positive.

Yet the real highlight of the weekend, for me, even more than the play, was when Frankl spoke. It was the evening before the play, and the auditorium filled up with students and intellectuals as well as a mixture of others. I don't remember details of what he said. But as clearly as if it were yesterday I remember one stunning moment. During a question and answer time a young man stood up and asked: "Do you believe in euthanasia, Dr. Frankl?" Since euthanasia was not a common topic of interest at that time, most people probably viewed the question as abstract or purely intellectual.

An awesome quiet filled the room. Frankl, who was a short, thin, but very imposing looking man with piercing blue eyes, drew himself up to his full height. His facial expression became severe, and the quietness persisted.

"I think if you know my experiences in the camps, you will know what I feel about euthanasia," he replied in essence. "I do not believe in it." His voice was dignified but authoritative and left no hint of opportunity for debate. The fact that the question itself seemed to be an offense to Frankl highlighted the depth of his conviction on the subject.

During World War II and before, Dr. Frankl had lived, not only with the attempted genocide of the Jews, but with medicalized killing of the elderly, the deformed, the hopeless in a prewar society in Germany which was aiming at perfecting the ideal race and eliminating all "useless eaters," those whom we would now call people with poor quality of life. Frankl had seen the "slippery slope" in action, and to me his body language, even more than his words that day, was unforgettable. The image of him standing there is forever burned into my memory.

We in the Judeo-Christian tradition give at least lip service to the preciousness of life. As Americans we talk a lot about the rights of individuals. But for me few moments have been as pregnant with the meaning of life as watching this brave man declare the value of a human life. After losing his family, his medical practice, and a precious manuscript to the Nazis, he had the credentials to speak about the value of life at its worst. His declaration of meaning had the stamp of authenticity. He had been where many people might choose death over life. Many did. Many in the camps killed themselves, hopeless regarding any future. But he had not only chosen life, he had embraced it and he had made others wish to embrace it as well.

On that memorable evening in Berkeley, the audience was composed of many far left, vocal students who loved debate. But something in Dr. Frankl's manner as well as what he had suffered forbade debate. A few years ago the world heard of his death. But the word that will always characterize him in my mind is *Life*.

Even when you are chased by those who seek your life, you are safe in the care of the Lord your God, just as though you were safe inside his purse! But the lives of your enemies shall disappear like stones from a sling!

—1 Samuel 25:29 (*The Living Bible*)

- 16 -

WONDER YEARS

A large frog toy box named Herbie sits on one side of my counseling office. To my adult patients he probably looks a little ridiculous. After all, how many family counselors have a green frog sitting in their offices?

But to those who are young, he is magic, for each child chooses a toy from Herbie before he or she goes home. For some it has gone so far that the child actually calls the treat itself a "Herbie."

Herbie is a toy box. Only that. Nothing more. But just the other day a slightly nervous child who met me for the first time turned to Herbie as if reassured by his presence and said, "Goodbye, Herbie, I've enjoyed meeting you." If things go according to plan, next week the little boy will say "goodbye" to me and will forget Herbie, except to get his toy.

These early childhood years are truly wonder years. They are a time when creativity is fostered, imagination is nurtured and we human beings learn what it is to dream dreams. They are precious years, which we cannot afford to waste or underestimate. Their potential is not limited by socioeconomic status, but cultivating this sense of wonder in any child does take some time from significant adults in his life.

In my own childhood my mother used to read me stories by the hour, and at night she would often tell me about her childhood on a farm in Wisconsin. I heard about taking cattle to pasture, searching for Indian arrowheads and trying to stop runaway horses.

I learned about ideals and ethics from stories which were deeply etched upon my mind. I began to form my own dreams for the future and I felt deep support for those dreams from parents who obviously felt I was important enough for them to spend time with me.

In my office, as children grow older they start complaining about the merchandise in Herbie. The toys are "junk" or too geared toward boys or towards girls, depending on whether a boy or girl is speaking. Others feel that the toys are not as interesting as they used to be and that they need to be replaced.

Finally, there is nothing left in Herbie for them. A few perceptive souls admit they've just grown up, but most think that the toys are now chosen with only younger children in mind and that their quality has deteriorated. A few children who are reluctant to give up on Herbie completely take a pencil or a key chain, methodically, as though they are trying to be polite.

And then even they quit Herbie. The wonder years are over. The child is grown. And how much potential for wonder remains in the emerging adult will depend largely on how these wonder years were spent.

※

Shade of the prison-house begin to close
    Upon the growing Boy,
But He beholds the light, and whence it
    flows,
    He sees it in his joy;
The Youth, who daily farther from the east
    Must travel, still is Nature's Priest,
    And by the vision splendid
    Is on his way attended;
At length the Man perceives it die away,
And fade into the light of common day.

                — William Wordsworth

- 17 -

NO THROWAWAY YEARS

A well-dressed, attractive woman sat in a doctor's waiting room alternately clutching the handle of her walker and nervously opening and closing her leather handbag. Just once she turned and nervously smiled, but otherwise she looked sad and unsure of herself.

In the background the nurse telephoned a convalescent home to make sure that they were giving her the proper medication. At the same time the nurse asked how she would be able to get back to pick up her eyeglasses. Would someone be willing to do that, she asked. In the meantime the lady in the waiting room looked down and fidgeted as she heard her needs discussed within hearing distance of everyone else who was waiting.

I looked at her again as she spoke to the nurse. She made sense. She even looked relatively young. When she got up to walk, she used the walker. But she was steady and walked rapidly as she left the waiting room. "Why wasn't she in her own home?" I wondered, or at least in the home of a relative or friend. Did she really need a convalescent home? Did she need such total care that other people needed to talk about her in front of her as if she were not even there?

I thought of my own mother at eighty, living in her house by herself, barely able to walk but thoroughly enjoying the dignity and independence of handling her own affairs. Her dogs, Cinder and Jackie, frolicked around the yard, and her roses bloomed as radiantly as ever. She loved to go out for dinner or to a store, but she always went back to her place, her home.

Then the accident had occurred. But even with a broken hip and ankle she had a more clear memory than others who had been in the same car. And she still looked much younger than her age.

But now the statistics she hid so well in normal life were starkly apparent on a medical chart. She was old. She was eighty.

"Be sure to put her back in the rest home where she came from," said a doctor we never met before, who looked older than my mother.

"She never has been in a convalescent home," I replied.

"Well, anyone over eighty ought to be," he said as he limped off down the hall.

Now, years after what turned out to be a fatal car accident, my mind went back to an earlier time when as a student I had lived with a Chinese family. Birthdays in that family were always important and none of us were ever forgotten. But the memory that stands out most in my mind was the time when the oldest lady in the family turned sixty. According to Chinese custom at that time, age was revered and honored, and sixty was a milestone toward real respect. I still remember the beautiful pearl ring she received to commemorate the event.

In the western world we stigmatize age rather than commemorate it. We try to hide age with cosmetic surgery and excessive makeup. The old imitate the young, leaving the young with no one worth imitating. Then we wonder why teenage suicide increases along with an increased feeling of uselessness among those who are aging.

Biblical truth differs from all this, for in the Bible old age is given as an incentive for obedience, not as a curse. Furthermore, throughout the Bible age is revered. The biblical pattern is not to wish for death as soon as the first indication of aging is perceived, but rather to embrace age as a time of special mentoring of the young and as a period of unique intimacy with God. As such it is a period of respect.

The German philosopher Goethe has an often-quoted saying which states that if we treat people as if they are already what they are capable of being, then we help them to become that. If we treat aging with respect, we help the aged to respect themselves and we insure that as we ourselves age we too will act in a way which will inspire respect.

Old age is not a time of throwaway years. In life there are no throwaway years. Old age is a Jimmy Carter building houses for the needy. Old age is Ronald Reagan writing a letter which will forever inspire the world as he slipped into the shadow of Alzheimer's. Old age is Mother Theresa ministering to the poor until God called her Home. Old age is sharing memories, listening to those who have no one to hear, imparting advice from the experience of years, forgiving because so much has been forgiven. Old age is a gift from God.

※

For age is opportunity no less
Than youth itself, though in another dress,
And as the evening twilight fades away
The sky is filled with stars, invisible by day.

— Longfellow (*Morituri Salutamus*)

– 18 –

STARTING AT THE END

Rose knew all the extremes of life. Born into a rich European family, she was raped and abused as a child. In her early childhood she was waited on by servants, dressed like a princess and given all the toys she could ever want. She was well educated by tutors and trained to be well mannered in every way. Yet she was never loved very much by parents who put her needs last in their lives.

Then when circumstances changed, as an older child she was given up to a European immigrant who settled in New York and cleaned houses for a living. In these homes where an orphan child was considered a liability, she was forced to eat actual scrapings from the plates of the rich. From the pampered childhood of her home she was now a poor orphan child in a strange new land. Eventually, marriage offered an escape and gave her great wealth once again, but not happiness. She had the servants, and now she had jewels instead of toys, but as before she was a toy, a plaything rather than someone who was loved.

For a few years in midlife she found love from a second marriage where she was valued and respected. But then she lost everything when her husband died unexpectedly. She became angry with God and erected a wall around herself. She was friendly but always guarded.

For the rest of her life she was frugal, but she always maintained the refinement and class of her birth. Her clothes, while old, always looked well kept up and attractively put together. A piece of fine silver or crystal made her entertaining seem special. Impeccable manners and good taste made her an enjoyable companion for an occasional musical event and dinner out. Yet she seemed always a little displaced: too poor to keep up with those whose interests she shared and too cultured to enjoy a coarser lifestyle.

Then one year before her death in her late eighties, she found God. For the first time she wanted a Bible. She asked for prayer and offered prayer for others. At last she could say "I love you" to those who loved her. In Christ she found the personal value she had never known before. In Christ she found eternal life. He had been seeking her all of her life. Now she had found Him.

Sometimes life is measured, not in years, but in months and weeks and days. Sometimes the end is simply the beginning.

I fled Him, down the nights and down the
    days;
  I fled Him, down the arches of the years;
I fled Him, down the labyrinthine ways
  Of my own mind; and in the midst of tears
I hid from Him…

(For, though I knew His love Who followéd,
    Yet was I sore adread
Lest, having Him, I must have naught beside)….

"Whom wilt thou find to love ignoble thee
    Save Me, save only Me?
All which I took from thee I did but take,
    Not for thy harms,
But just that thou might'st seek it in My
    arms.
    All which thy child's mistake
Fancies as lost, I have stored for thee at
    home;
  Rise, clasp My hand, and come!"

— Francis Thompson

- 19 -

The Rescue

He was no novice. As a sheriff working for years in a small town, he knew where to draw the line between firmness and compassion. On that afternoon in September, as he walked into the prisoner recreation room, the warm stuffiness made him feel that tinge of claustrophobic oppression which is so much a part of general prison life.

Going over to the old-fashioned wooden windows, the sheriff started to push one open. As usual, the window stuck from the heat of the day. Pushing a little harder, his hand slipped; and before he could get his balance his hand had gone through the thick glass and his body had jerked back, landing him flat on the floor.

For a moment he was stunned. Then a stabbing pain shot up his arm and the blood gushing on to the floor beside him brought into focus the reality of his desperate situation. For all practical purposes, he was alone, helpless, with no one who would care near enough to hear his cries. Surrounded by a group of hardened criminals who viewed him as the enemy, he made a feeble attempt to drag himself to the door. No one attempted to help.

Just then a prisoner ran over and crouched down beside him. The sheriff felt his own revolver slide out from beneath him. Then the young prisoner held the other prisoners at bay with the sheriff's revolver, now fully cocked. With his free arm he dragged the bleeding man toward the outside door. With quick dexterity he managed to take the sheriff's keys, open the door, drag him outside and then relock the door—all in seconds. Then giving the gun and keys back to the sheriff, the young man ran for help. Lying there on the floor bleeding, the sheriff wondered if help would come in time. Then, mercifully, he passed out into oblivion. Hours later in a hospital recovery room the sheriff awakened to tell his story.

For both men, in an instant life itself had taken on a preciousness beyond that which either man had felt before. One man had almost lost his life. Another had broken an unspoken rule of conduct among his peers and in so doing had put his own life in jeopardy. Yet each man had found his life. Beyond his own rescue, the sheriff had realized the preciousness of all life, even among those whom he had thought had little or no value. The prisoner was released from prison for his act of valor. But his greatest reward was his knowledge that in a crisis he had chosen to save a life, even at the risk of his own life.

Because he clings to me, I will deliver him...

— Psalm 91:14 (*New American Bible*)

- 20 -

MOST PRECIOUS POSSESSION

At thirteen life had started to get complicated for Robert. His face had broken out with acne and in his mind even the kids who didn't tease him probably thought he looked pretty ugly. His grades had gone down over the course of the year and he wasn't very happy with himself or life in general.

Walking home from school one afternoon, Robert felt especially hopeless. As a friend ran to catch up with him, Robert decided to tell him how he felt. "Do you want to come to my house to hang out?" Robert asked, thinking that this would give them a chance to talk. "I can't," responded his friend. "I've got a music lesson in forty minutes." Robert just looked indifferent and kicked a small rock a few feet ahead of him.

When Robert reached home, he decided to bluntly tell someone he needed to talk. On the kitchen sink he found a plate of cookies, carefully covered with a plastic wrap. By it was a note from his mother telling Robert that she'd be home later after doing some errands. One of his sisters had gone with her. That left Bonnie, who was home on break from college, and David, who was still in high school.

Robert knocked at Bonnie's door. "What is it?" she shouted.

"Can you talk?" asked Robert.

"I'm on the phone. Can we talk later?" responded Bonnie.

"Sure," said Robert, trying to act like he was fine. "Nothing serious."

Robert found David in his room with earbuds, listening to music. David didn't even see his brother as he shrugged his shoulders and walked back down the hall.

Once back in his room Robert began to build on the events of the day: a failed math test, a rebuke from a teacher for not paying attention, and now nobody who even seemed to notice him.

Slowly, he took out a small pen knife which he had gotten for Christmas: "What would it feel like to die?" he wondered. "Would anyone even care?" Gingerly he opened the knife and gently rubbed the blade across his wrist. Then, a little harder. His wrist began to hurt and the skin wasn't even broken! Maybe this wasn't the right way to go. Yet the sight of the blade mesmerized him. It gave him a sense of power where before he had felt completely powerless.

At that moment Bonnie came in to tell Robert she was off the phone and wanted to talk. Then she saw the knife in Robert's hand. For a long moment they were both silent. Then Bonnie began to cry.

"Robert," she said, "I'm so sorry. I didn't even know you were this upset. Please tell me next time. Then I'll know." Suddenly Robert's emotions shifted and he didn't feel so alone. After all, his friend cared about him and couldn't help he had a music lesson. And his mother had left cookies – actually, his favorite cookies. As Robert and his sister talked, Robert began to realize that for a few low grades and some pimples which would go away some day anyway, he had almost given up his most precious possession, his life.

※

To ease another's heartache, is to forget one's own.

— Lincoln

- 21 -

SMALL THINGS

Flying home on a commuter plane one Monday afternoon, I turned to see one of the most exquisite sunsets I have ever observed. Across a darkened sky the sun flashed a brilliant red hue. Underneath was the shoreline of the Pacific Ocean. And moving in like a lacy veil was a storm cloud of black fog. For a moment I was struck silent with awe. Then, turning to an older businessman who was seated next to me, I said softly: "Look out the window. It's beautiful."

Patronizingly, he looked, nodded and smiled faintly. For a brief moment I felt a little like a small child pointing out a new, marvelous discovery to a bored, adult world who had seen it a million times before. But, I continued to look and drink in the sight that would remain a long time in my memory in spite of coming home to asphalt streets and rows of concrete apartment buildings.

It occurred to me then, as it has so often since, that we are so acutely affected by the small things in our lives. Somehow we survive the catastrophes, the deaths, the severe illnesses, the sharp reverses in fortune. We brace ourselves and get through. Usually at these times we have great emotional support from friends and family.

Yet most of the fabric of our lives is composed of little things. We are discouraged by a word of disapproval from a friend or the moodiness of a store clerk. A fretful baby, a leak in the plumbing or a car that runs out of gas two blocks from work is enough to set a whole day into negative course. Nor do we get much sympathy at these times. The dramatic receives attention; not the small, ongoing needs of life.

Yet if small events discourage us, a smile from an unknown passerby or a thoughtful compliment over a small task well done can make our whole world seem right again. For most days are not filled with crises but with the everyday trivia of living. If we focus on the positive trivia of the day rather than the negative we will find that our lives are changed rather dramatically.

For me as I came home that day, the view of the sunset out of the plane window was just a small thing, but it lifted me up just as the dampening mood of my companion somewhat subdued my enjoyment. Then, as sometimes happens in life, my experience ended on a positive note because of another insignificant event.

The pilot's voice interrupted the quiet of the plane where most passengers were engrossed in their evening paper or asleep over their briefcases.

"I hate to intrude upon you," he said, "but please turn to

your right and look at that sunset over Monterey Bay. Never in all my flying have I seen anything quite so magnificent." Most people looked passively and turned back to their own thoughts. The man next to me looked a little harder and then gave me a warm smile of understanding.

※

Horizon, reach out!
Catch at my hands; stretch me taut!
Rim of the world,
Widen my eyes by a thought.

— Leonora Speyer

- 22 -

THE RED GERANIUM

A colleague once told me of a patient he had been seeing who had lived for years on high wires. His health run down, he had finally sought professional help. After several months of therapy, one morning the man suddenly commented on the beauty of a red geranium that was blooming outside the doctor's office. "It's always been there," my friend replied. "You've just never noticed it." Seeing the red geranium was the first indication the patient gave of real progress toward normal living. For the first time in years, the man had literally stopped long enough to smell the flowers.

Even if we are not actually living on a high wire, sometimes we don't realize how fast we have been going. My encounter with the ocean following a surgery once again helped me put my life into perspective. I was physically weak and in some pain. Worst of all for me, my thinking was foggy from the anesthesia and pain medication. I had planned to use this time of recuperation for thinking about book ideas and organizing my current writing schedule. If I couldn't see my patients, I had naively assumed with the ignorance of one who has never before had major surgery that I could at least have more time to write and think about writing. It didn't work that way, and for the first time in a long while I had to be content with doing nothing.

Three days after surgery I slowly put a day's effort into walking outside and up some stairs at my motel to a table surrounded by lawn chairs. Exhausted by the exertion, I relaxed into one of the chairs and looked out at the ocean in front of me. This time the sea was bright blue and the sky was sunny. A couple of sailboats drifted by slowly. The moderately high waves, tipped with foam, came in toward me and then disappeared from my view under the grassy cliffs. The cycle repeated itself with a kind of hypnotic monotony. Farther out, the sea looked blue and calm, stretching back into a sky that seemed to come down to meet it. Overhead, the sea gulls flew back and forth, like choreographed beings used as stage props to enhance the beauty of the sea and to add their sounds in a kind of symphony with the waves.

As I watched the scene, I realized how long it had been since I had really *seen* the sea. I thought I had watched it. Certainly it had uplifted me often. However, not for years had I just sat quietly and absorbed its beauty – not looking for inspiration, not looking for anything really. As I slowly made my way back down the steps toward my room, I realized that the sight of that blue ocean, always there, always the same, had quieted my restlessness.

I tried to use the time of my illness for productivity, and I found that instead I had been forced to stop altogether. Yet, strangely enough, the time had not been wasted at all. I had seen the majesty of the sea and had reflected on the One under whose control we all remain. When once again I returned to my work, it was with a sense of renewal that I had not known in a long time.

We are never safe, but we have plenty of fun, and some ecstasy. It is not hard to see why. The security we crave would teach us to rest our hearts in this world and impose an obstacle to our return to God: a few minutes of happy love, a landscape, a symphony, a merry meeting with our friends, a bath or a football match, have no such tendency. Our Father refreshes us on the journey with some pleasant inns, but will not encourage us to mistake them for home.

— C. S. Lewis

- 23 -

JUST TO BE

When I was twelve, my mother and I went back to our old home in Chicago for the summer. It was a time of sight-seeing and visiting relatives. On a hot Sunday afternoon, my mother and I went to Great-Aunt Christine's house for a small family reunion. I was the only child present and at first I felt a little left out.

The house was a lovely old structure, well kept up and impeccably furnished. All the chairs had white lace doilies and the tables had ruffled doilies under the lamps and vases. Everything was starched, and clean, and perfect. In the middle of it all was Great-Aunt Christine, with her white hair softly rolled up on top of her head with a perfection that equaled that of the house. The relatives sat drinking coffee from finely decorated china cups, and the conversation flowed around me.

"Would you like a glass of cold grape juice?" someone behind me asked. It was my Great-Aunt Christine's son, Warner Sallman, who had painted the well-loved head of Christ. He was probably the only famous person there, but to a child he was more impressive for his kindness than for his paintings. I don't remember what else he or anyone else said after that, but I do remember that I suddenly felt part of this large group of people of varying ages. A cousin whom I didn't really know had drawn me into the group. Even though I didn't know most of them, they were my family.

Someday I would be adult like them and drink coffee from china cups instead of grape juice from a glass. Someday I would be respected and honored like Great-Aunt Christine. I was part of a whole, and for the moment at the center of that wholeness was an elderly lady whom I would never really know personally but whom I would never forget. On that hot afternoon so long ago, all that was needed was for her just to be. For me that was the unique function of her old age.

※

White hair is a crown of glory and is seen most among the godly.

— Proverbs 16:31 (*The Living Bible*)

- 24 -

POSITIVE RAGE

Responding to a book on anger which I once wrote, a friar monk wrote to me. He had hesitated with regard to his final vows because he felt he had to be totally free of anger before he could take them. Interestingly enough, it was the scriptural references in my book which convinced him that anger was not a sin and he was okay.

Taken one step further, Christians are vulnerable to depression because we tend to feel so guilty about ever feeling anger. We deny the anger and lock it up within us and then are surprised when it comes out as depression or when it turns into some bodily ailment, like an ulcer. The Bible says: "Be angry but do not sin; do not let the sun set on your anger…" (Ephesians 4:26, *New American Bible*). The Bible tells us *how* to be angry; it does not forbid anger.

At the other end of the cycle, as a counselor I often talk to people who are in varying stages of depression. One of the signs of breakthrough which I look for is anger. A show of anger means that the depression is beginning to weaken in its hold on the person. Often depression is the result of anger turned inward. When a person understands the source of his or her anger and begins to deal with it in a positive way, depression is on its way out.

When we misconstrue God's teaching and deny a healthy expression of normal feelings of anger, we end up with other negative feelings, like false guilt and depression, which, when they escalate, can cause everything from mild unhappiness to that final giving up – suicide. Action is one way to defuse both anger and the resultant sense of depression. Jeff is a good example of this principle.

Jeff kept pulling the trigger on the loaded gun he had pointed against his head. He was only twenty-five, but he had learned the meaning of despair the night his wife ran off with his best friend. After that, he had spent most of his time drunk. Now even drinking didn't dull the pain. Depression alternated with rage. But increasingly depression was winning. Time after time, as he stood outside in the darkness, Jeff pulled the trigger. Repeatedly the gun wouldn't fire.

Not wanting to live, and seemingly unable to die, Jeff went to a nearby phone booth and called one rehabilitation center after another and asked for help. The answer was the same: no openings. Yet something within Jeff kept making him push on. If he died, he wouldn't get another chance at life on this earth. He didn't want to give up on something which might turn out to help him.

Finally, one center agreed to put him on a waiting list. The man on the other end of the phone gave out one other ray of hope, however: "Call," he said. "Call every day. That way they'll know you're serious."

For days Jeff lived to make that phone call. Actually, most days he called many more times than just once. Calling became the focus of his life. Gradually, he forgot about dying and fought to live. Depression gave way to anger and a fierce will to live. Jeff finally got into the center, and today he is a happy, functioning human being.

Hopelessness builds upon hopelessness. When it becomes the focus of our thinking, it gets bigger and bigger, like a giant snowball rolling down a hill. Hope, however, when mixed with action does the same thing in a positive direction.

※

> Be ye angry, and sin not: let not the sun go down upon your wrath...
>
> — Ephesians 4:26 (*King James Version*)

- 25 -

SMALL OCCASIONS OF RELIEF

It was a misty, overcast day. Here and there dense black clouds threatened to turn the soft drizzle into torrents of rain. As if in response to the uncertain atmosphere, traffic on one of the most crowded of all California freeways moved more slowly and less predictably than ever. It was, in general, a good day to stay home! Yet with a sense of illogical logic that such was the pathway to tranquility, my friend and I battled the elements and the Los Angeles freeways to meet a third friend for tea. We had planned this escape for a week; in recent days, the pressures of life had been unusually heavy. Now, no inconvenience of weather, distance, or traffic jams was going to stop us from a much-needed break.

As we drove off the freeway and down the coast toward the hotel where we were to meet our friend, even the ocean appeared gray. Yet as we approached the hotel and watched the waves washing up over the beach below, once again, as always, the sea began to have its calming effect on me.

To complete the scene, the hotel lobby, with its great bowls of flowers and its crackling fireplace inside, added a contrast of cheerfulness to the gray skies and the turbulent sea outside, a contrast I have always found to be enormously uplifting. The knot in my stomach relaxed, and I no longer felt in a hurry. The safety zone of afternoon tea with good friends in a relaxing atmosphere was beginning to have its positive effect.

As we waited to be seated, a lady in front of us turned to her friend and said, "This morning I felt in such turmoil I knew that if I didn't plan this I wasn't going to make it." Her friend smiled understandingly and agreed that she, too, had known such days.

The friend we came to meet was late. She was the only one of us who didn't have the day off, and so she was rushing to get away from work as early as possible. After some time went by, a telephone message was relayed to us explaining that she was late but on her way.

Enjoying the luxury of a whole day off, I felt a twinge of guilt. If you rush too much to get to a place of relaxation, that place itself can become just another high wire, another demand that adds to rather than detracts from the demands of life. I thought that perhaps I should call my friend and tell her that we understood if she couldn't make it, but I didn't have her work number with me. So we waited.

We finally sat down while our tea steeped and continued to wait for our friend. I looked out the windows at the sea, and once again I felt the tranquility of the scene: the sea outside, the warmth inside, and the serenity of just doing nothing. Steeping tea cannot be hurried. It takes its time, no matter what the immediacy of the situation. Maybe that's part of what makes taking tea have such great potential for providing a safety zone of comfort, a place or time of refurbishment. It slows us down. It forces either contemplation or conversation.

Then I looked across the room and saw my friend approaching. "This is just what I need," she commented, with the conspiratorial smile of one who has escaped in spite of many obstacles. "I'm so glad I didn't give up on coming," she said, and I was glad I hadn't called and discouraged her. The three of us had all needed a safety zone that provided a break from the everyday pressure. We didn't need, nor could we take, a vacation in the south of France, but we did need that minibreak that can make, in a cumulative way, the difference between going on and burning out. If burnout can come in small increments, so can relief be provided by many small occasions of relief.

> Whenever anything momentous occurs, whether matter for celebration or tragedy, a pot of tea is produced. When friends meet unexpectedly, they exchange news over tea.
>
> — Helen Simpson
> (*The London Ritz Book of Afternoon Tea*)

– 26 –

Gingerbread Boys

They were called gingerbread boys then. Not gingerbread boys and girls. Certainly not gingerbread persons! With their raisin buttons and jaunty frosting hats and boots, they were every inch male.

The year was around 1945. It was Christmas. At school, plans were being made for the class Christmas party. Impulsively I volunteered my mother's Christmas cookies. Predictably, she came through for me. I knew she would!

But she didn't just make cookies. She made gingerbread boys – twenty-nine of them! Each one looked fat and proud, just ready to burst his plump raisin buttons. They had faces and clothes, all outlined in colored frosting. Each one was covered carefully with a clear wrap and became a small Christmas gift for every member of the class.

Most of the children just looked at these creations for a while before they bravely broke off a foot or gingerly nibbled at an arm. It was the 1940s; it was a time before the proliferation of commercial cookies and elaborate, gaudy decorations. For most of my classmates, this was a major treat. It was unusual.

A cookie is not a big thing. But all these years gingerbread cookies have stood out in my mind as important. I was the star of the class for a day. And best of all, deep down inside I knew my mother cared a lot to go to all that effort. She had not only come through on my promise, made on her behalf; she had outdone herself. It was a concrete proof of her love. It was evidence of the importance of the small things in life.

If a child asks his father for a loaf of bread, will he be given a stone instead?...Of course not!... won't your Father in heaven even more certainly give good gifts to those who ask him for them?

— Matthew 7:9-11 (*The Living Bible*)

- 27 -

Love Letters

It was a Sunday afternoon. I was nearing the end of sorting through countless papers and boxes after the death of my mother. The last box of papers lay in the corner of my mother's bedroom, so insignificant that I was tempted to get sloppy and throw it away. But I opened the box anyway and found it was filled with letters written almost daily by my father during the last three months of 1941 while he was away in Seattle working for Lockheed Aircraft Corporation. My mother must have kept them by her bed for those long seven years following his death. They were a comfort which she had not even shared with me.

They were loving letters sent from a husband to his wife against the backdrop of the bombing of Pearl Harbor, the start of World War II, rationing and constant blackouts, and my father's work involving national defense secrets.

Packing and cleaning were suspended as I spent the rest of the afternoon reading those letters. My first reaction was that of a daughter, tears of loss and feelings of pride and love. But as I continued, I saw in my father's letters a combination of love and authority at work. It was a mixture which is both biblically and psychologically sound, a blending of affection and order which is spoken of much in the church and in the counseling office, but which is seldom exemplified or understood in real life.

Part of the difficulty with the institution of marriage in this country today is the unspoken implication that a good marriage is an instant, automatic state. If immediate harmony and bliss do not result, the marriage is not considered successful.

Marriages may be made in heaven, but the working out of any marriage is definitely done on earth in a life-long process of growth. It takes work, and the desired result is balance.

As I read my parents' letters that Sunday afternoon, I understood on a gut level the divine balance of the authority of the husband blended with the biblical injunction to the man to love his wife. I saw my parents, not so much as my parents, but as two people in their early forties, very much in love and very involved in growing in their personal lives and as mutual heads of a family.

The line between respect and love is a fine one, for real respect tends to issue forth into at least some form of love. Love each other they did. And what was nice were the clear expressions of that love. They each wrote daily, which in itself was a declaration of love. My father wrote of cutting holly and sending it to my mother's sisters. At another point, when he was temporarily in San Diego and was allowed home for a brief time, he wrote that he would take the train home since "I don't want to take the plane (although it is safe) because I know you will worry about me." Concern about people's feelings in the seeming trivia of life is sometimes the greatest expression of love.

But love was expressed openly as well. He usually X'ed his letters with kisses and at times closed his letters with sentences as maudlin but as real as, "I hope I'll see you in my dreams." The one thing my parents never lost in their marriage was romance.

Perhaps our culture in its obsession with sex has forgotten what the sexual act represents – a union of love. Intimacy is more than a physical act. It was for my parents a daily sharing on paper; it was reflected in my father's gift of perfume when there was no money for perfume; it was expressed in the sharing of homey details, like my father's favorite walks down by the ships during his childhood in Sweden. They argued and disagreed at times; but underneath, that first flush of romantic love never faded to the day my father died.

Such love is not too idealistic in even such a tarnished world as our own. As a child growing up I experienced all the frustrations and disagreements with my parents that any other child has. It was not a perfect family; we were not perfect individuals. But never once did I ever doubt my parents' love for me. And never once did I ever doubt their love for each other. I rarely questioned who was "boss" because their opinions tended to blend. "They" – a sort of corporate being – were "boss." Their relationship was one of their greatest gifts to their children.

As I said goodbye to the earthly remains of my mother, I stood by her casket and thanked God that He had ever given her to me and ever so gently committed her to the earth until that day when we shall be caught up together with Him.

And so in a sense it was the final relinquishment of both my parents. If that is true, it is appropriate; for in life they were one, and that oneness gave them forty years of a marriage which for the rest of my life will keep me from disillusionment with God's potential for marriage, in spite of what I see around me.

We are shaped and fashioned by what we love.
— Goethe

- 28 -

Freedom

As I was sitting under a temporary canopy autographing books, several of us were chatting. It was a bright, sunny day, a seasonal parenthesis in the middle of a rainy spring. As I glanced over the landscape of the college campus which had been engaged for the weekend, for as far as I could see there were sweeping green lawns and large shade trees.

Across the way in the distance the crowds were assembled in a circular pattern focused on a small platform of dignitaries. Flags from various Scandinavian countries fluttered in the wind, adding a touch of color to the landscape. In between that group and myself small tent-like booths had been erected to serve food, while other booths dotted the landscape selling various ethnic articles, like wooden shelves, Christmas ornaments, dolls, cookware and paper goods. Resembling a medieval festival, people dressed in native costume as well as in normal American clothes perched on various shady slopes, some eating and others playing with their children. Children with cotton candy and various carnival-like toys ran up and down the grassy slopes.

Suddenly, I realized that the crowd had grown still, and a

man was singing the American national anthem. Many had risen to their feet. A few yards away from me a plain, middle-aged lady dressed in a red native costume stood with her hand over her heart, softly whispering the words of the song. The people I saw were not in that inner circle around the platform. Their attention was not required. I myself could not even see the platform from where I sat at my booth. But for as far as the ear could hear these words of freedom, the quietness and reverence were maintained. This was a crowd full of immigrants and their families. They had chosen the freedom inherent in a democracy. For them that freedom was precious.

Is life so dear, or peace so sweet, as to be purchased at the price of chains and slavery? Forbid it, Almighty God – I know not what course others may take; but as for me, give me liberty, or give me death!

— Patrick Henry

- 29 -

An Orange, a Photo, an Email

It was a simple picture of an orange tree which started it all. Our family had moved to California from Chicago when I was three. After the war when gas rationing was gone, we all started traveling once again. The extended family could connect in person instead of just by mail. One summer a close cousin of my mother's and her family came to visit. I was about eight, while the cousin's two children were older.

Burton was the oldest, and to me he was awesome in his handsome Navy uniform and his friendly manner. As he told his sister later, we were "buddies" during that visit. So while my older sister and Muriel engaged in teenage interests, I, the little kid who would have been left out and bored, did fun things with this sailor-cousin who understood a child.

Years later as I had been working on scrapbooks, I found a special picture which brought back all of the memories. The picture was of Burton on a ladder in our backyard, picking oranges which he handed to me as I stood on the ground. Coming from the Midwest, my parents were especially proud of the fruit trees in our backyard. Visiting relatives and friends responded accordingly. And citrus fruit seemed to top the list of reasons why living in California was like living in a paradise, so to speak.

As I looked at this particular picture, a flood of happy memories came back of what we did on that visit so many years ago: walking through the outdoor Farmer's Market, which is still a favorite spot for me; my staying up late while our parents reminisced; listening to Muriel playing her guitar. But most of all I remember Burton, in his handsome Navy uniform.

All these years later, when I found the picture I had already been renewing my relationship with Muriel over family history and photos. But I had never again talked to Burton. I had just started to learn how to use the Internet, so I asked her for Burton's email address. Then on divine impulse I sent him an email with the picture of the two of us and the orange tree, and thanked him for all those past memories. I had a book deadline and a new office to find, but for some reason I didn't wait until later.

On July 25, 1999, Burton emailed me back. He had not felt well, he said, but seemed better and was working on a picture to send back to me. That was at 4:38 p.m. By 11:30 p.m. on that same day, even though she had talked to him the previous day, Muriel tried to reach him and never did. Burton was now with his Lord. Burton had died sometime after he sent that email. Except for his email to me, Burton could have died any time after late on the 24th when Muriel had talked to him. But this email record narrowed the time down so that we know that his death was not prolonged.

When I heard of Burton's death a whole group of thoughts went through my mind: an orange, a photo, an email. A chance to remember and say good-bye for now. A sister who didn't have to question how long her brother might have been alone dying. A reminder that modern technology like the Internet can be used for good as well as evil. It was a striking wake up call that it's never too late to say "Thank you" – and, as Joan Rivers would say, "Do it now."

※

Let the dawn of every morning be to you the beginning of life, and every setting sun be to you as its close; then let every one of these short lives leave its sure record of some kindly thing done for others, some goodly strength or knowledge gained for yourself.

— Ruskin

- 30 -

The Price Tag of One Life

It was late at night in the spring of 1944. The Nazis had begun their purge of Hungarian Jews, the last large intact group of Jews in Europe. A handful of neutral nations, Sweden in particular, were trying to save as many Jews as possible. But now those efforts had become more complicated. With the heightened Nazi presence in Hungary coupled with the Jews being forced to wear the yellow star in order to make them stand out as Jews, every Jew's life was in danger as never before. On one of the first days that Jews appeared on the street with the yellow star sewed onto their garments, a knock was heard on the door of the young second secretary of the Swedish Legation. As the thirty-two-year-old Swede, Per Anger, opened the door he saw a friend, a Jewish businessman, Hugo Wohl standing there in the darkness. The man was obviously agitated as he stood covering with his passport the huge yellow star which was sewn on to his clothing.

"Come in! Come in!" said the Swede as he motioned to the man and closed the door simultaneously. The relationship between the two men had been primarily that of trade between Budapest and Sweden. It had involved two men of equal standing working together and respecting one another. Now the businessman was pleading with the diplomat. "Per, you must help me!" he said.

Per's mind went back a second to the immediate past, the day when he walked out into the streets of Budapest and saw for the first time multitudes of Jews wearing bright yellow stars on their clothing which marked them as Jews, "life unworthy of life." In the words of another Swedish diplomat, Lars Berg, the star cried out: "I am a Jew. Treat me as you like. Beat me; deport me; rob me; send me to the gas chamber. I am not a human being, just a Jew." Per felt their loss of dignity deeply. Now he felt that loss even more acutely in the friend who stood in his residence.

His next thoughts were desperate. He was a diplomat from a neutral nation, but what difference did that make now? What could he do to save this man which was any more effective than what he had already been trying to do?

Then gradually an idea began to formulate in his mind. He routinely issued provisional passports to Swedish citizens who had lost theirs. That was a normal function for any foreign embassy. Hugo Wohl was not a Swedish citizen, but still maybe those provisional passports could save his life, and if his life, why not the lives of his family members and even other Jews?

Per Anger was a correct, career diplomat. Years later he

became an ambassador. He was kind, gentle, bright, but he was not used to breaking rules. Until now he had functioned within prescribed guidelines. A decision to break rules now could cost him his career. It could jeopardize the well-being of his wife and his soon-to-be-born baby. But to obey the rules could also jeopardize the very life of this man who stood before him.

"They can fire me," he said out loud. "But I have to do this." Hugo Wohl and his family were given the Swedish provisional passports. And eventually others too were saved in the same way.

Later that year another Swede, Raoul Wallenberg, joined the original six Swedish employees of the Swedish Legation in Budapest. He took the idea of using the provisional passports and transformed them into a more elaborate document called the Schutz-Pass, with the golden emblem of the Swedish crown and the picture of the person to whom it belonged. It looked official and appealed to the detail-oriented mind of the Germans. The Schutz-Pass was often called "the paper of life and death." It officially declared the protection of the Swedish government to the point that toward the end of the conflict in Hungary, the Swedish Legation on the hill overlooking the city began to be called the Jewish Embassy by those who were thwarted and angry in their failed efforts to eliminate all Jews. By the end the Swedes and their comrades had saved one hundred thousand Jews.

The effectiveness of Swedish passes, however, started that one night in the spring of 1944, when a young Swedish diplomat decided that his whole career was not worth the price tag of endangering the life of another human being. Although it was not on his mind that night, he also learned that one person truly can make a difference.

Occasions do not make a man either strong or weak. They only show what he is.

— Thomas A Kempis

- 31 -

THE GOOD REPORT

In the Old Testament before the children of Israel entered the promised land, God commanded Moses to send spies into Canaan to see what the land was like. Their report was good: the land flowed with milk and honey. It was a good land.

A number of years ago as my father lay on a hospital bed close to death, he was asked how things were with him. He replied succinctly, "It is the grace of God which has brought me thus far, and it is that grace of God which will bring me through." He gave a good report of that Land to which he was going.

I remembered years before when as a child I used to hear him recite his favorite biblical passage, the Twenty-third Psalm: "…though I walk through the valley of the shadow of death, I will fear no evil: for thou art with me…" Now, close to the time of his departure to be with his Lord, the report was still good. In a few last moments of life he had given me a priceless gift. His words encouraged me more than anything else at that time. They were his truest legacy to his children. The Land to which he was going was okay; we didn't need to fear aging and death.

The end of a thing is the test. It was our Lord's rejoicing in His last solemn hour, that He had done the work for which He was sent. "I have glorified thee on earth." He says in His prayer, "I have finished the work which thou gavest me to do; I have manifested thy name to the men whom thou hast given me out of the world." It was St. Paul's consolation also, "I have fought the good fight, I have finished the course, I have kept the faith; henceforth there is laid up for me a crown of justice, which the Lord shall render to me in that day, the just judge."

— John Henry Newman

- 32 -

Early Arrival

When I invite someone to my house, on rare occasions they come early. Now, we're not talking a little bit early. We are talking *early* on a grand scale. The vacuum is out. My hair is still wet. I'm dressed in a robe. And dinner hasn't even started to cook! Usually when someone is this early, they've just mixed up the time altogether.

Even a little early is disconcerting, however. Dinner is okay, but I'm not. My hair is still wet, since that's the last thing I do. And I haven't got my dog situated so he can't lunge and bark at the first, to him, intruder who enters the house.

A Christian who commits suicide must create a similar scene in Heaven. You're right. Heaven won't be unprepared in the same way as we are. Heaven is perfect, while we live in imperfection. But you can count on one thing. If it's not your time, Heaven won't be ready for *you*. Personally, I'm sure you can stay. After all, we're saved by faith in Christ.

Remember, though, that "…faith without works is dead." (James 2:26, *New American Bible*) So be sure that your faith was real.

To commit suicide is to break one of God's most ancient

commands: "Thou shalt not kill." It transgresses against God's will when He says: "'Obedience is better than sacrifice…" (1 Samuel 15:22, *New American Bible*) Suicide fails to recognize that God who counts the hair on our heads also counts our days, our hours, our minutes.

If you decide that you know better than God when your life should end, you will be arriving early in Heaven. Furthermore, you won't have done everything on earth which you were put here to do. You'll never teach that class, or pray for that person who needs you, or share Christ with that person who doesn't know Him. Who will do it for you? I don't know. I just know you won't have obeyed God's complete plan for your life. You will have arrived in Heaven before God called you.

※ ※

Teach us to number our days,
that we acquire a wise heart.

— Psalm 90:12 (*Darby*)

- 33 -

I'll Never Again Be Anyone's Child

When I was a little girl I remember lying down one afternoon to take a nap, my mother beside me. I was never good at sleeping during the day, so I lay awake and turned to look at my mother who was already fast asleep. As I looked at the wisps of soft brown hair curling around her temples, and watched her facial muscles relax into a deep sleep, I experienced perhaps the first pangs of anguish I had felt in my short life. I caught my first glimpse of mortality. Someday she would pass from the earth. The human body would be no more. She would die.

As I grew through childhood and became an adult, death did not occupy much of my thinking. But even so I began to learn that every death that affects us has its own uniqueness. When my twenty-two-year-old girl friend died, I realized in a profound way that even the young die. But still, death had not touched the very foundations of *my* life.

Now, from my own experience as well as what others have shared with me, I know that there is a uniqueness in the death of a parent, especially both parents. For no matter how old we are or how early we "flew the nest," there is a deep, uniquely precious bond with one's parents. They knew us at a time few people now remember; they knew us in ways no one else ever did. Irreplaceable memories are connected with these people which can never be totally understood by anyone else. Childish secrets that were shared; tiny fears, made big by the darkness of night, quieted by a parent's touch – such is the fabric of a child's memory of these two (or one) significant persons in her life. It's no wonder that when they are taken, a part of us, too, is gone.

When my father died, I felt loss, grief, and a considerable sense of having my foundations shaken. Seven years after my father's death, my mother died in a car accident. Since I was the youngest in a close-knit family of elderly aunts and uncles, most of whom had died since my father's death, I was left virtually alone.

I also believe that there is a uniqueness in the death of the last parent. The day before my mother's funeral I felt terribly empty, with what psychologists call "free floating anxiety." I groped for a way to identify the feeling, but its vagueness only made it harder for me to cope. Then I began to re-read a book, *The Summer of the Great Grandmother* by Madeleine L'Engle, and my eyes caught one line which illuminated all of my feelings: "I will never again be anyone's child." That was it. That was what I was feeling. Although I had been an adult for many years, now there was no turning back, not even for a moment.

Later as I talked to others who had lost parents I realized how universal was the feeling *I will never again be anyone's child*. But for me on that bleak Sunday afternoon, knowing that one other person had felt as I did helped me to start my recovery. A simple sentence had explained my seemingly complex emotions.

No matter what methods one uses, recovery from any painful experience takes time. One must be gentle with oneself and not rush. For in some ways, it's not the quick, crushing blow of death which hurts the most. It's the little things which come after. For me, once again I felt this most deeply after my mother's death. The worn slipper which somehow isn't found at first, but later brings back a pang of grief; the pet dog which looks with innocent, inquiring eyes as if to ask what has happened; the unmailed letter or half-finished handiwork; the old, the worn, the familiar; there are a thousand such reminders. One reminder can trigger a chain of memories, "what if's," guilt feelings, and regrets which can build into days of anxiety and depression. But we have a choice. We can shed tears and go on. We can turn off the build-up of emotion and refocus on something positive and concrete.

It was an old garden glove which did it to me. I found it in my mother's art studio under a chair long after her personal belongings had been disposed of. There it was, sandy, worn, well-used. I looked out the glass doors and saw the roses flourishing, the trees bearing fruit – and I cried. Then as my thoughts began to go off in every direction – to the details of the accident and past memories – I stopped crying and went home. All of that had been felt and expressed before. It was best for me to go on.

※

Our little systems have their day;
>   They have their day and cease to be;
>   They are but broken lights of thee,
> And thou, O Lord, art more than they.

— Tennyson

- 34 -

Angels Unaware

Last week a young man came into my counseling office determined to talk about something he had never told anyone before. It took him thirty minutes to reveal himself, and to him it was the hardest thing he had ever done.

Most people feel that their secrets are unusual, never before experienced, perhaps worse or more painful or more sinful than anyone else's secrets. Yet usually they are variations on a not too uncommon theme. Most of the time the person who reveals them feels better for having shared, as long as they share with someone who understands. What this particular young man revealed was a tragic happening in his own life, but nothing he should have felt compelled to conceal all these years. Yet when he left he made the poignant statement: "Thank you for being so safe for me."

When we deal with each other, we are dealing with beings who possess immortal souls. We are interacting with persons made in the image of God. We are walking on sacred ground. The man who told me his innermost secret was trusting me with himself at his most vulnerable point. He was trusting me to be safe.

In this trust God has given to us in dealing with each other we never know the nature and the depth of another person's vulnerabilities. A middle-aged woman on welfare had some disabilities as well as a number of deep emotional scars from childhood. As Christmas approached each year her pain increased as she longed for what had never been. As a child she had always wanted a Christmas stocking. Then when she was nine her parents had promised her one which would be filled with treats if she was good. She tried very hard. When on Christmas Eve she hung up her stocking, she went to bed eager with excitement. The next morning she ran to get the stocking and then stopped in horror. Inside was a switch to whip her with, some rocks, and a note which said, "You weren't good enough."

Years later a person who knew her distantly decided to make her a stocking. The friend knew nothing about the childhood stocking, but she did sense that the woman had few friends and little money.

The stocking itself was beautiful: red with lace trimming and a golden angel embroidered on the side. Considering this project a gift toward God's work, the friend filled the stocking bountifully: a good pen, a pair of warm gloves, a tube of lipstick, maple sugar, a gold pin, a small book, a key chain, some candy and a big, super-sized gingerbread cookie. It was done tastefully and expensively, as one would do it for a family member or close friend. It was worthy to be given to one who was created in the image of God.

The woman's reaction was a total surprise to the friend. First she told her about the childhood stocking. Then she said: "At first when you gave it to me I was scared. I tried not to think about it out of fear that it would change into something bad."

Then, she continued, came Christmas morning. "I was speechless. I felt I had experienced my first Christmas. Now I understood what it meant to experience love, joy, wonderment – the spirit of Christmas."

The friend never knew until then what a great gift of love she had given when she gave this woman her Christmas stocking.

Often we are unaware of the specific needs around us. But God has a way of leading us even when we don't see the whole picture. It is then that almost unaware we become ministers of love in meeting needs which we may know little about. It is by providing safety and care for our fellow human beings that we truly recognize their importance before God. In this way we validate their worth.

Let there be something true and fine
When night slips down, to tell
    That I have lived this day of
    mine
Not selfishly, but well.

                            — Edgar Guest

- 35 -

ONLY EIGHTEEN HOURS

He only lived for eighteen hours. The fight to save him was lost. A waste of technology, you could say. He was buried in an unmarked grave; a small brass disc with a number designates the location of his tiny remains. I never could find the exact spot, so instead of leaving flowers I brought something home instead: a small pine cone from a tree in the general location. I keep it on my computer desk to remind me of how precious eighteen hours can be.

He missed his first birthday. He never went to school or summer camp. He never slipped into the cool water of a lake on a hot summer afternoon. He never wrote a book or sang a song. But then, too, he never sat at his grandfather's grave, or broke his arm in a fall from his bike, or watched his family split in two – or three or four.

Yet he lived, and still lives on. Part of that great crowd of Believers of Hebrews 12:1 who watch us from afar, he cheers us on like one member of a large crowd rooting for his team in the last inning. Joining with similar experience that group of the unborn who live in Heaven, perhaps he understands and supports and cheers us on with a slightly louder voice because he had those eighteen hours.

※

Teach us to number our days aright...

— Psalm 90:12 (*New American Bible*)

- 36 -

IMAGES ON EASTER, 1999

An old man with a drawn, pale face leans heavily on his wooden staff. Then his face crumples and his head drops into his hands.

A young woman lies on the ground dying, murmuring: "I can't get air. I can't breathe." Then she turns her head and is silent.

A child, healthy enough for the moment, wails into the vastness around him, not expecting an answer or comfort, just needing to express his terror.

On a dirt road, set apart from the thousands of other refugees, a child of about two years of age just stands alone, looking around for some familiar face, then darting ineffectively a few feet in each direction. She is lost at the edge of a sea of lost human beings.

"Refugees," "Genocide," – the words always inspire detached regret and sometimes a sense of obligation to correct what is wrong. But at the end of the twentieth century, on the week commemorating the death and celebrating the resurrection of the Prince of Peace, images from Kosovo become flesh and blood to those who see them daily on the television screen or on the front pages of newspapers and magazines around the world. For pictures give life to words.

Each image of each person represents a real life and is, therefore, precious. The old have not finished their time with their grandchildren. Some have not completed their life task. Most expect to live a little longer.

The dying have not yet said their goodbyes. Indeed some, with a shot of penicillin or a simple medical procedure, would not be dying at all if they were in another place or time.

And the young – what about the young? Some are so young that they are as vulnerable to death as the very old or the very sick. Those who are a little older have at best lost their childhood. But to a child fleeing for her life simply because of who she is, innocence is forever dead.

These images of refugees fleeing from genocide are images of how precious life gets for those in danger of losing their lives. These are the faces of Kosovo on Easter 1999.

※

You have seen me tossing and turning through the night. You have collected all my tears and preserved them in your bottle! You have recorded every one in your book.

— Psalm 56:8 (*The Living Bible*)

- 37 -

Pink Clouds

Otto Frank, the father of the legendary Anne Frank, once said that while his daughter and he were close, he never really knew her until he read her diary after her death.

Years ago as I thought of his comments, I reflected back on my own childhood, on what was truly important and what was not. I thought of my own granddaughter and wondered how well we in the adult world, no matter how much we loved her, really knew her, even at five years old. Then I reflected on my years of working with teenagers, both as a teacher and a counselor, and I asked what I have always asked: "How do I get far enough into this young person's thinking to influence and help them?"

The most important thing my Uncle Dave did for me was not when he left me a small inheritance, although I valued that. But what I will always remember is when he and Aunt Gussie met my mother and me in the train station in Chicago when I was twelve. A two-night, three-day trip on the Santa Fe's *El Capitan* had left both my mother and me tired. Worst of all, I had walked alone into the restroom in the middle of the night to find a woman lying on the floor in a pool of blood. By the time we arrived in Chicago, I just wanted to go back to California, to my father and pets and friends. In short, I was traumatized and homesick but not very verbal about my feelings.

Uncle Dave was the one who really caught on. He was my mother's oldest brother. He and his wife had never had children. But during the weeks we stayed in his home, he understood a child better than most adults who had their own children. He truly gave me the gift of time, and we were inseparable. We went to Lake Michigan where he taught me to fish, and he showed me how to play tennis. By example he taught me the important lesson that to help someone you have to start with where they are.

As time went on the nightmare of the trip diminished and my confidence came back up. By the time we left to go back to California, I wanted to stay in Chicago! A relative who on some level understood the needs of a frightened child had made the difference. Time and understanding had worked a cure which money could never have bought. I doubt that he ever fully comprehended how I felt and how much he had helped. But somehow he did all the right things. After my mother and I returned home, a few days later a brand new tennis racket arrived: a gift from Uncle Dave. I still have that tennis racket. It symbolizes a precious memory of understanding.

Children are naturally greedy. They long for a new toy and

clamor for the newest candy or trinket at the checkout stand in a supermarket. But inside of them they have a pretty good value system, a remarkable sense of what is important. In the visitation which accompanies most divorce settlements, as a regular practice many kids would rather spend real time with the weekend parent than be handed a wad of money and left at an amusement park. Most kids want to be heard by an adult who is significant in their life. And a great number of young people prefer the sentiment behind a gift more than its monetary value.

A teenager who passionately wanted a certain pricey designer outfit was ecstatic when her father sent it to her. Then when she found out that his girlfriend had found the outfit and paid for it as well, she put it away and refused to wear it. Her comment? "He really hasn't changed, has he?" The gift was valueless without meaning.

Yet for all the times children verbalize their feelings, and for all that we adults understand just because we were once children, Otto Frank was right. Frequently we really don't know. But now and then we get a glimmer. One evening years ago my then five-year-old granddaughter called me over to a window in my living room. "Look!" she exclaimed. "Pink clouds!" The sight was beautiful as some puffy clouds had mingled with the sunset and for the moment looked like mounds of cotton candy or strawberry snow cones. I wondered how many "pink clouds" she saw and we adults miss in this world which is so new to the young and so taken for granted by us.

※

Treasures

His overalls hung on the hook by his hat, and I
    noticed his pockets were bulging out fat.
So I emptied them out in a pile on the chair, and I
    tenderly touched every treasure with care:

There were three rubber bands, a parking lot ticket,
Two paper clips and a fishing cricket,
A camphor ball and an empty match box,
A half dozen nails and a couple of rocks,
A yellow golf tee, two lollypop sticks,
A marble, a spool and three tooth picks,
A knife and a pencil, some dry corn silk,
A wire and a cap from a bottle of milk,
A rusty door key and a white chicken feather,
An old clock gear and a piece of leather,
A flash-light bulb and three or four strings,
A broken dog biscuit and two hair springs.

Then I gathered them up, all his "treasures" so grand
    —ev'ry rock, ev'ry nail and each rubber band,
And I put them all back, then I kissed him good-night,
    And he smiled in his sleep as I turned out the light,
And I thrilled as I thought of the fun and the joy
    such trivial things could give to a boy.

                      — Author Unknown

- 38 -

A Different Clientele

In a hospital bed, an old man lay dying of an unknown disease that had baffled the staff. "He's senile," said one doctor. "He doesn't understand what we're doing." Then as they roughly tore off his sheet and began to examine him, he resisted them, and they gave up defeated and disgruntled. A nurse watched the scene quietly and waited until the doctors left. She put the man's teeth back into his mouth so that he could talk, and she spoke warmly to him. She treated him as if he were *not* senile, and she found out that indeed he was not impaired in any way intellectually. Finally he explained his uncooperativeness. It was simple. He didn't like being examined rudely and roughly. He wanted the dignity of an explanation. She talked with him for a while and then, at the staff meeting, explained his feelings. "I guess we'll have to explain each step," the physician involved said in an irritated tone of voice as he left the meeting. Yet the result of that nurse's concern was cooperativeness by the patient, which led to better treatment; an easier time for the physicians, who didn't have to fight the patient's resistance; and a patient who had regained his self-respect.

In a day when specialization isolates and patients have

become numbers in a computer, a regard for the dignity of each human being is even more important than ever when it comes to medical treatment.

Sometimes patients' needs for respect are met unexpectedly well. An elderly woman was called before dawn and notified of her husband's death. The incident occurred during an energy crisis, and so the streets were dark as were the halls of the hospital.

But as she made that painful last visit to her husband's bedside, she noticed that the lights by her husband's room at the end of the corridor were turned on. Some of the gloom disappeared from a very hard moment because a nurse anticipated the psychological impact of darkness at a time of death.

In another instance an older woman wandered into a medical building looking for help. She spoke little English and was on state aid. Her family wished that she had never come here from Europe. A kindly person who happened to meet her in the hall of the building went with her into several offices to see if they would treat her. With politeness, and in one case without politeness, she was turned down. At the last office they tried, the doctor agreed to see her, money or no money. But the doctor went one step further; she came out into the waiting room where the woman was sitting alone and said, "I would be most happy to be your doctor if you would like me to." She didn't accept her grudgingly. Rather, she treated her with the same dignity she would have given a paying patient.

As we move into the ever-changing medicine of the future it is important to remember the sacredness of life and the dignity of all human beings.

※

The great psychiatrist Dubois once said so rightly: "Of course one can manage without all that and still be a doctor, but in that case one should realize that the only thing that makes us different from a veterinarian is the clientele."

— Viktor Frankl, M.D.

- 39 -

The Martyr

Two teenage boys were on a rampage of death in a school where because of them no one else was safe. Somewhere the boys had lost their way in life and now to them life was no longer precious. And so, they began to shoot. As a student sheltered his sister's body with his own so that he would be shot instead of her, and as other students tried desperately to save a teacher's life as he slowly bled to death, the shooters went on killing. The sound of gunshots was punctuated by laughter. Silence was merely a prelude to more sounds of explosives. To those students who hid in terrified quietness, life had never seemed so precious—or so vulnerable.

"Do you believe in God?" one teenage shooter asked a girl as he brandished his gun, ready to shoot.

"Yes, I believe," answered his schoolmate.

"There is no God," the shooter retorted. Then the shot came, loud and final. The teenager he killed was instantly in Heaven with her Saviour Jesus Christ. She had joined that group of martyrs of Hebrews eleven of whom it was said the world was not worthy.

Real martyrdom never minimizes the value of life, it affirms it. It has been said that he who has nothing to die for has no reason to live. Life is so precious that it requires a meaning which exceeds mere earthly existence.

Real martyrs don't want to die. Suicide is not martyrdom. Yet martyrs still exist. They are often discovered in unusual ways and unlikely places. On what started out as an ordinary day a young girl in school made an extraordinary choice. She said "Yes, I believe." In so doing she gave up her earthly plans and dreams for God who was even more precious to her than her life on this earth. She became a Christian martyr.

Finding, following, keeping, struggling,
Is He sure to bless?
Angels, martyrs, prophets, virgins,
Answer, Yes!

— Stephen the Sabaite (725-794)

- 40 -

The Safety Zone of Christmas

Last year as I once again looked forward to celebrating Christmas Eve, I paused to reflect. All the preparations for the traditional Swedish smorgasbord were completed except for the final serving of the dishes, which ranged from pickled herring and potato sausage to the Christmas cookies, cut into their various festive shapes and sprinkled with colored sugar. Red candles were lighted all over the house, and in its usual place in the dining room stood my little tree with its colored lights which my father bought me when I was four. And again, as in every past year, my favorite thing was the big tree in the living room. The toy ornaments, the old colored balls from the past, the tin ornaments from a memorable time in Mexico: all these gave me that warm feeling which is a result of a pleasant blending of the past and the present. But most of all there were the lights: small twinkling lights, icicle lights, colorful bubble lights and, this year, a new addition: running lights which created the illusion of small white lights literally running all over the tree.

The night seemed so comfortingly familiar. Memories from childhood flooded my mind: waiting for the aunts and uncles to arrive; knowing that I would always go to bed in new pajamas that night; eating the special foods which had been prepared for days before; and, the highlight of the evening, opening gifts. When I was a child, Christmas Eve was a magic night of dreams come true. Then, after all the festivities of the Swedish Christmas were over, in true American style I, like children all across this country, would fall asleep hoping to catch a faint sound of reindeer landing on our roof.

Even on the Christmas that fell a week after my father was buried, the small, modestly decorated tree and the evening of modified smorgasbord and small gifts shared with family and friends provided the comfort of the familiar and reminded all of us of the true meaning of Christmas. The realization of the miracle of Christmas, God become Man, increased my awareness that my father had joined that great cloud of witnesses in Heaven. His last words on this earth which were known to us were, "It is the grace of God which has brought me this far, and it is the grace of God which will bring me through." Those words in themselves were a comfort.

Actually, that year, when the poinsettia plants reminded me more of funeral decorations than of the celebration of Christmas, the meaning of Christmas as a time of rejoicing in God's greatest gift to mankind became more real to me than ever. Christmas became a safety zone, a refuge from the pain inevitable to human existence, a place of comfort.

Well over half a century has gone by since those first childhood Christmases in California after my family moved here from Chicago. It is over fifty years later, and yet it seems like yesterday; the Swedish tradition of celebrating Christmas on Christmas Eve, Americanized in many ways both for convenience and preference, has remained with me. It provides a point of stability in my life each year. It carries with it memories of Christmas past which cannot be taken from me. It has become ever-expanding in its potential for change within the basic structure which remains for Christmas present. It is one of the safety zones in my life.

> Dark and dull night, flie hence away
> And give the honor to this day
> That sees December turn'd to May.
>
> — Robert Herrick

- 41 -

THE STRANGER

It seemed to be just a chance meeting with an elderly lady on the sidewalk of a small town in the country. A friend and I had gone there to spend a summer afternoon, walking along the quaint, tree-shaded streets and making small purchases in a few of the stores. The stranger appeared, like the two of us, to be spending her time just looking at store windows.

We smiled, and she asked me about my dog Horace. Horace barked amiably, enjoying the attention. We chatted a bit, but I don't even remember much that was said. Her looks, too, like the conversation, were not outstanding. She had ordinary white hair pulled back into a simple knot. Her clothes were plain but neat. Yet from her face emanated a glow of joy and a look of contentment which distinguished her from other passers-by.

My day in this country town had been a small attempt to make up for vacation plans which had fallen through, a time of rest and change which had been desperately needed. I had been discouraged and weary. Yet somehow the cheeriness and inner joy of this stranger, whose name I never did know, were contagious. I felt myself renewed just from my brief encounter with her. It had been a short outing that day. The encounter had been even shorter. Yet those few moments had been precious, at least to me. Then, as if to reinforce the importance of this seemingly trivial piece of life, before we went our separate ways, she mentioned her "Lord." And I knew our meeting had been no chance meeting at all.

※

When once Thou visitest the heart,
Then truth begins to shine;
Then earthly vanities depart;
Then kindles love divine....
Thee may our tongues for ever bless;
Thee may we love alone;
And ever in our lives express
The image of Thine own.

— Bernard of Clairvaux (d. 1153)

- 42 -

Reaching Earth

Last winter I spent a long weekend by the ocean. It was one of those times of ideal, refurbishing retreat that occur infrequently in most of our lives. Combining good friends, a small but meaningful worship service, and the backdrop of a rugged, scenic coastline, the weekend provided a safety zone in the middle of heavy demands. The peak of enjoyment for me was an unexpected afternoon spent at the old Point Loma lighthouse.

The view from the lighthouse has been called one of the three greatest harbor views in the world. On the day of our visit, the fog was thick and the wind brisk. As I walked up the steep hill to the lighthouse I had a sense of peaceful exhilaration. Then the lighthouse itself came into full view, perched high above the earth with one sole function: to throw light into the darkness in order to warn ships of the rocky coast below and to direct them to safety.

I learned that after it was built the keeper of this lighthouse was responsible to have the lighting equipment in good order by ten every morning so there would be no chance that the light would fail to shine each night. Wicks were trimmed, lenses cleaned and polished; for otherwise the light produced by the whale oil would not show through. All this had to be accomplished at the beginning of the day, not in a hurry right before the light became necessary.

An interesting detail about the Point Loma lighthouse is that it was built high on top of a hill so that it would more effectively cast its light over the sea below. But because it was so high above the earth, sometimes the fog rolled in between the ocean and the lighthouse, obscuring the light. For that reason a new lighthouse was built on lower ground and the old Point Loma lighthouse became a tourist attraction.

We cannot live too closely to God. We cannot reach too high above the earth to God. However, many Christians tend to disconnect themselves from practical problems of earth. Like this lighthouse, at some level there is a disconnect from earth. We don't like to see the unpleasant. Yet it is impossible to change this world and act in love toward those in need if we stay in our safe little neighborhoods and never see real, live, hurting human beings.

A friend of mine often remarks about a "bag lady" she encounters almost every time she goes grocery shopping or anywhere else around town. The sight of this lady always disturbs my friend, but up to a week ago that was as far as it went. Then last week she dropped by my apartment after work and enthusiastically said: "I saw the bag lady again." Not perceiving anything of particular interest in her statement, since she always seemed to see her, I made some casual comment in response.

"You don't understand," she continued. "I decided I couldn't just go by and pretend she wasn't there. So I went over to McDonald's and bought a cheeseburger, some fries, and a carton of milk. Then I went back and gave them to her. I found out her name and we talked."

Now thoroughly interested, I asked, "What did she say?"

"Not much," my friend said. "But she seemed surprised when I asked her name. And as I left I looked back, and I noticed that she was no longer hunched up, looking down at her feet. She had picked her sweater up off the sidewalk where people could walk on it, and she was sipping her milk."

The light from the lighthouse had reached the earth and had penetrated one small corner of the darkness.

In him was life, and the life was the light of men. The light shines in the darkness, and the darkness has not overcome it.... The true light that enlightens every man was coming into the world.

— John 1:4-5, 9 (*RSV*)

You are the light of the world. A town [or a lighthouse] on the top of a hill cannot be hidden. Nor do men light a lamp to put it under a bowl; they put it on a stand, and it shines for all in the house. So your light is to shine before men, that they may see the good you do and glorify your Father in heaven.

— Matthew 5:14-16 (*Moffatt*)

- 43 -

UNTROD TERRITORY

Several decades have gone by now since I stood with my mother at the bottom of a long gangplank and waved "goodbye" to an older couple, dwarfed by the size of the huge ship as they stood on the deck waving and smiling back. The scene became etched in my memory for life because somehow even then I knew deep inside that this time they would not come back.

Perhaps the couple felt this too. Only recently I found an old letter from them, written from where they were in Canada, telling of their travel plans home to England. It contained a poignant request: "We hope to make a brief call at Los Angeles on this ship. Please note that on July 3rd we will be arriving at 8:00 a.m. and leaving again at 2:00 p.m. the same day. It would be such a joy to us if you could call at the dock and just say 'hello!' and 'goodbye!'" It was not a request they had made before.

For years Alfred J. Crick and his wife Margaret had come from England to hold Bible studies which I attended. With his wife he had endeared himself to many, not least of whom were small groups of young people scattered here and there who learned how to do real Bible study from him. I remember one occasion when my parents and I took them to the ocean for the weekend, and Mr. Crick and I had a chance to take a long walk by the harbor, both talking, his answering my questions.

Now my mother and I were at another harbor to say "Goodbye." As I stood there I wanted to remember what they looked like on that bright crisp day. For me it was the end of a very important mentoring, a very special friendship. It was a transition.

It is hard to face the impermanency of life. Yet in the constant change which we automatically encounter we are reminded that change is inevitable until that final transition into eternity.

Change means new and new is always scary. If the change is devastating, then it is obvious why the experience creates fear. The loss of a loved one, the loss of a job, sudden poverty, a loss of medical insurance: all of these changes will obviously produce fear.

But even good change can create anxiety simply because it is new. I am just moving into a new apartment as I write this book. It's in the location I wanted. It's the right size. It's the right price. Yet as I move I'm a little anxious. Why? I really can't tell you in any definitive way. But it's new and therefore unknown and scary.

When I was very little and went to the dentist with my first cavity, I remember his saying right before he gave me a shot of painkiller: "This will hurt a little but it won't last. Then you'll start feeling numb." I braced myself. But because he had warned me, the event was no longer completely unexpected. The pain was not as bad as I had anticipated. The process had been explained. The unknown had become more known and therefore the fear had diminished.

A man who helped train me to be a therapist once told me that every time he traveled and ended up at a new hotel, he always explored the place thoroughly before settling down. That way he made the unfamiliar familiar.

Yet often life presents changes which cannot be explored prior to experiencing them. They are either thrust upon us without warning, much like an earthquake or a tidal wave, or they cannot be understood until they are experienced, like being in an airplane for the first time or being given general anesthesia. Then regardless of whether we feel dread of what we decide is bad change or joyous anticipation of what we perceive as positive, we approach the new situation with tinges of uncertainty simply because it is totally new.

Many years have passed since my mother and I stood and waved at those loved ones on board ship. Not too long after, they were both with their Lord. My mother has now joined both of them in Heaven, and I believe that from that more distant vantage point they all still wave and cheer me on. For all of them the transition to Heaven was a good one. It was the great and final transition, and once in Heaven new was no longer scary. For me who was still on earth, the time ahead was untrod territory. It was new. And since the changes which occurred took place on earth, not in Heaven, they were still scary and took a little longer to adjust to.

I tell you a truth hitherto kept secret: we shall not all sleep, but we shall all be changed, in a moment, in the twinkling of an eye, at the sounding of the last trumpet; for the trumpet will sound, and the dead will be raised incapable of decay, and we shall be changed.

— 1 Corinthians 15:51 (*Weymouth*)

- 44 -

The Lesson of the Tide

It was during several vacations in Mexico that I realized most fully that a whole host of situations in life cannot be eradicated. As a child, for example, going to a doctor meant to me that one would be automatically well. Then a little friend of mine died from polio, even though her father was a doctor. When I was in my teens I was hurt in an automobile accident. As I waited for the ambulance, I remember a kind man bending down saying, "We never think that this can happen to us." And I didn't think it could. But it did. I kept having flash thoughts that this had to be just a nightmare and I would soon wake up.

Yet throughout my early life I held on tenaciously to the notion that a problem could always be conquered, eliminated, done away with. Injustice could be abolished if we worked hard enough. The impossible just took a little longer, as the saying goes. Disillusionment came at times when my theory failed, but I rationalized it with the thought that the next attempt would be successful.

Somehow in Mexico the beginning of realism broke through upon my thinking. It's not that I became less idealistic. For more than ever before I believe that God can indeed do the impossible and there is no person alive in whom God cannot perform miracles.

But now my idealism is at last becoming temperate. Each time I stayed for any amount of time in that tropical climate I was totally defeated by the onslaught of mosquitoes and my allergy to them. Coming from Southern California, where heat is eliminated by air-conditioned cars, homes and stores, I now found myself in a much hotter climate grasping gratefully for purified ice cubes. I looked around and saw hunger that was not satisfied, animals that suffered without a Society for the Prevention of Cruelty to Animals, death unsoftened by funeral homes, and lives which could not be dramatically altered.

In the United States we have easy answers for many problems. The government subsidizes our poverty and takes care of us, to a degree, in old age. We have instant food, microwave ovens, immediate news coverage from all points in the world, sophisticated medical treatment and, in general, many comforts that most of mankind has never even dreamed of. Yet even for us, and at times especially for us, the basic problems of mankind like loneliness, physical pain, depression and anxiety can still not be eradicated. To believe otherwise is to be disillusioned.

Tonight I walked down by the ocean and watched the tide

as it moved relentlessly in and out over the smooth shoreline. The softness of the rocky beach was evidence of the fact that the tide always does go back and forth. It never stays out and it never fails to return. So it is with our feelings. Painful and joyful, they do not stay static. They leave, they return. And part of the gracefulness of maturity is to know this fact. For no matter how painful things become, the feelings do not remain; yet neither can they be eradicated. Pain in one form or another returns. But again, only for a time. What does remain forever is the One who is God and the host of heavenly beings who surround us with love and care.

His Presence does not guarantee the eradication of need, whether the need be emotional, spiritual or material. But He does guarantee that needs will be met.

Things at their worst will either
   cease, or else climb upward
To what they were before.

— William Shakespeare

- 45 -

Messiah

Flying at dusk from the Mexico City airport to a small coastal town, I felt like I was being thrust into another world, another era of time for a brief period. We were a little late. No one else seemed concerned. There were six of us on the plane, all speaking Spanish except for me. A lady across the aisle quietly began to nurse her baby, and a small boy tried to sell me a newspaper I couldn't read.

I turned back to look at the lady with the small infant. I watched her as she tenderly stroked the child's face. Her eyes gazed admiringly at the tiny hands that clutched at her clothes. She and the baby were absorbed in each other, and each appeared content. I wondered who this child would be when he grew up. Perhaps he would be too poor to get an education. Maybe poverty would limit his whole life. On the other hand, with the abundance of love that was apparently his, a good self-image might also be his and could well be valued above the fortunes that most people so frantically seek.

That night in the small village where I stayed my impressions were further deepened. Houses without walls, dogs with only bones showing through their skin, people living and dying within a small radius of where they were born; it was very remote from the world I knew.

The next afternoon I fidgeted in the afternoon sun, looking for something to do, and watched everyone else sleeping peacefully through the heat. I began to wonder how much these people were really missing. Many of them had done hard labor in the morning, but knew when to quit in the tropical heat of the afternoon. In the cooler weather of evening I saw fathers playing lovingly with their children. I saw older people with their families gathered around them.

In the short time I was there, my own expectations, to put it into Thomas Carlyle's words, were reduced to zero. I didn't miss modern conveniences that much. Ice cubes, pure water, the ocean, and good friends seemed all that were essential. Yet too much of today's world is instilled in me for me to forever leave my work and ambition for even this tropical paradise. And so as I returned to this country and deadlines and schedules, Wordsworth's shades of the prison house began to close in.

To many of us today the meaning of success has deteriorated to power, fame and above all money. If it is true that you can, in part, judge a people by their television commercials, then it would be accurate to assume that our greatest gauge of success at this time is money. If you are rich, you are successful. We feel that if we are having a hard time financially we aren't "making it," and we have a compulsion not only to keep up with the Joneses but to surpass them.

Illustrating the same idea on an entirely different level, one Christmas I was deeply moved by reading about the composer George Frederick Handel. Throughout his life, Handel fought reoccurring indebtedness. At one point, he suffered from a paralyzing stroke which promised, at the age of fifty-two, to end his creative life. His spontaneous recovery from his paralysis has never been understood by doctors. Then, four years after his recovery, he wrote his famous oratorio, *Messiah*, finishing only twenty-three days after he started. As Handel stared at the bulky manuscript, he exclaimed, "I think that God has visited me!"

After its initial success, however, the *Messiah* seemingly lost its popularity. The organized church thought it was sacrilegious to speak of God from a stage rather than from the pulpit, and so the piece was effectively boycotted. Finally, after giving up on paying his debts with the piece, Handel gave it to London's Foundling Hospital, where to this day a handwritten copy of *Messiah* is on display.

Handel then began leading a yearly performance of the *Messiah* in the hospital's chapel. At first, people came to hear this man who was known to be the world's greatest organist.

But eventually they came to hear *Messiah*, until the yearly performance became the highlight of the London social season. Handel became blind in his sixties, but he continued the performances until his death at seventy-four. In the last years, when he was accompanied by children to the organ, the audience would cry in sympathy. As he began to play, they would weep out of joy.

Messiah has never stopped gaining in popularity since that day. Yet Handel never earned one penny from it. His greatest work was one which he gave away to a foundling home, and yet it marks the pinnacle of his success. Handel's debts have long since been forgotten. But the importance of his life can be summed up, at its highest level of achievement, in one word: *Messiah*.

If of thy mortal goods thou art bereft,
And from thy slender store two loaves alone to thee are left,
Sell one, and with the dole
    Buy hyacinths to feed thy soul.

                    — Abuslih-ud-Din Saadi

About the Author

A former high school teacher and school counselor, Elizabeth Ruth Skoglund is a Licensed Marriage and Family Therapist in private practice in Southern California. She is a certified bereavement facilitator for both adults and children. She is the author of over 40 books, numerous magazine articles, and a weekly newspaper column, and has appeared on many TV and radio talk shows. She has been named the Outstanding Scandinavian American 2006-2007 by the American Scandinavian Foundation of Thousand Oaks and was awarded Beautiful Activist 1973 by the Germaine Monteil Cosmetic Company and the Broadway Department Store.

Skoglund's books include: *Life on the Line*; *Safety Zones*; *Bright Days, Dark Nights*; and, more recently, *Secrets of the Second Half*; *Gifts From the Hearth*; *Found Faithful*; *Divine Recycling* and *Before I Die*. *Bright Days, Dark Nights* as well as *Burnout, Divine Recycling, Before I Die, I'll Be Better in the Morning* and *Life on the Line* are available on Kindle. Skoglund's website is www.elizabethskoglund.com. She can also be found on Twitter, Facebook and LinkedIn.

www.ingramcontent.com/pod-product-compliance
Lightning Source LLC
LaVergne TN
LVHW091255080426
835510LV00007B/272